I0153977

Atticus Greene Haygood

The Case of the Negro as to Education in the Southern States

.

Atticus Greene Haygood

The Case of the Negro as to Education in the Southern States

ISBN/EAN: 9783337366728

Printed in Europe, USA, Canada, Australia, Japan

Cover: Foto ©Suzi / pixelio.de

More available books at **www.hansebooks.com**

THE CASE OF THE NEGRO,

AS TO

EDUCATION IN THE SOUTHERN STATES;

A Report to the Board of Trustees,

BY

ATTICUS G. HAYGOOD,

GENERAL AGENT OF THE "JOHN F. SLATER FUND."

— —

ATLANTA, GEORGIA:

JAS. P. HARRISON & CO., PRINTERS AND PUBLISHERS.

1885.

Gentlemen of the Board:

The statistical statements presented in this paper are taken from official sources, as the United States Census Tables for the different years referred to; from documents sent out under authority of General John Eaton, United States Commissioner of Education; from the reports of the chief officers of the State school systems, and from the reports of the various benevolent societies engaged in the work of educating the lately "emancipated people" in the Southern States of the Union. The statistical exhibits in this paper are not confined to the Negro population nor to the Southern States. Important facts relating to other States and to the white race are brought into this discussion, as being helpful in the study of the special subject of your investigations. Wise conclusions as to the education of either race can only be reached by considering the facts of the education of both races. As an appendix to this paper, a number of statistical tables are added for convenience of reference in the course of the present investigation.

POPULATION AND DISTRIBUTION.

Table I gives the total population of the United States in 1880, showing its distribution by States, giving the number of whites and colored people, the area of the several States, and the density of population per square mile. This table takes no account of Chinese, Japanese and Indians—except as they are included in the totals—making a total of 172,-020, as shown on page 3, vol. 1., Census of 1880. Table II gives the number, nativity and race of the legal school population of each State and Territory in 1880. Of the whole population, 6,580,793 are people of African descent, the great mass of them being pure blood Negroes. Of the whole colored population 6,099,253 are found in the former slave States and the District of Columbia. In some of these States, as Delaware, Maryland,Missouri,Kentucky and West Virginia, the proportion of colored people to the population is much below the average. It appears that of 6,099,253 colored people in the sixteen late slave States and in the District of Columbia, 5,360,298 are found in eleven States—Alabama, Arkansas, Florida, Georgia, Louisiana, Mississippi, North Carolina, South Carolina, Tennessee, Texas and Virginia. In these States the white population is 7,622,-852. To understand the subject more fully, Tennessee and Texas should, for the moment, be taken out of the list, for in these States the preponderance of the white population is far beyond the average. Comparing the two races in the remaining nine States, we find of white people 5,286,784; of colored people 4,563,763. That is, of the whole colored population of the United States, 6,580,793—4,563,763 are crowded into the following named States : Alabama, Arkansas, Florida, Georgia, Louisiana, Mississippi, North Carolina, South Carolina, and Virginia. In three of these States, Louisiana, Mississippi and South Carolina, the colored people are in the majority.

If the rate of increase of the two races is maintained, the census of 1890 and 1900 will afford startling comparisons. Experts tell us that the increase of the total population of the United States,between 1870 and 1880, was 30.6 per cent.; the increase in the white population, enormously aided by immigration, was 28.82 per cent.; the increase in the negro population, unaided by immigration, was 34.78 per cent. Some writers on these subjects seek to break the force of these figures by calling in question the accuracy of the census tables, but these tables are the highest authority we have. Some offer their personal observation in evidence against the count of the Government! Some seek to prove a different and lower rate of increase of the colored race by comparing longer periods, as the decades between 1840 and 1860 and between 1860 and 1880. It were better to compare ten decades. We will find that from 1784 to 1884, the negro race in the United States has grown—using round numbers—from about 700,000 to 7,000,000. No form of words can intensify the argument that such facts maintain. In these facts lie the weight and urgency of the duty of using all wise means to educate these incoming millions of our negro population in all that will tend to make good and useful citizens.

THE FACTS OF ILLITERACY.

Tables III. and IV., taken from Circular "No. 3, 1884" issued by the Bureau of Education (the Tenth Census furnishes the material for these exhibits), contain the statistics of illiteracy, in 1880, for both the white and colored adults in the United States.

The Tenth Census shows in the United States, 937,235 adult colored people. Of these, 266,138 are in the Northern 114,694 in the Pacific, and 2,556,403 in the Southern Division of States. In 1880 there were of illiterate (that is, "unable to write") adult colored people 2,147,900, distributed as follows: in the Northern Division, 91,746; in the Pacific, 37,156; in the Southern, 2,018,998. The per centage of adult collored illiterates is as follows: in the United States, 73.1; in the Northern Division of States, 31.9; in the Pacific, 33.2; in the Southern, 78.9.

A further analysis shows of illiterate colored males "21 years of age and upward"—that is, of colored voters—a total in the United States of 1,022,151, or 68.7 per cent of the whole number; of illiterate colored women "21 years of age and upward"—that is, of the wives and mothers of the colored race—1,125,749, or 77.6 per cent of the whole number.

These illiterate colored adults were, in 1880, distributed as follows: in the Northern Division of States colored men unable to write, 43,533 or 31.8 per cent of the whole number; colored women unable to write 48,213, or 38.0 per cent of the whole number; in the Pacific Division, colored men unable to write 26,674, or 27.3 per cent; colored women unable to write 10,482, or 62.6 per cent; in the Southern Division, colored men unable to write 951,944, or 76.0 per cent; colored women unable to write, 1,067,054, or 81.8 per cent.

The urgency of the need and duty of wisely educating the colored people is greatly increased by the revelations of the same census tables of white illiteracy in the States where the illiterate colored voters, parents and children, make up nearly one-half the entire population.

In the States where we find 951,944 illiterate colored voters we find 411,900 illiterate white voters, or 14.3 per cent of the whole number of white males "21 years of age and upward." In the same States are 553,489 illiterate white women—wives and mothers—or 19.4 per cent of the adult white female population.

The percentage of illiterate white voters in the Northern Division of States is 5.6; of illiterate adult white women 7.7; in the Pacific Division, of illiterate white voters, 8.6; of illiterate adult white women, 12.1.

Tables V and VI, in Appendix to this paper, give the statistics of adult illiteracy for both races in the United States in 1870. Comparing these tables with tables III and IV, we find a relative decrease of illiteracy for the whole country—except the Pacific Division, in which there was both an absolute and relative increase of colored adult illiteracy. Thus: in the Northern Division we find, illiteracy of white adults in 1870, 8.7 per cent, in 1880, 6.6; of adult males in 1870, 6.7, in 1880, 5.6; of adult females in 1870, 10.7, in 1880, 7.7; in the Pacific Division, illiteracy of white adults in 1870, 13.7, in 1880, 8.6; of adult males, in 1870, 10.4, in 1880, 6.6; of adult females in 1870, 20.4, in 1880, 12 1.

The illiteracy of colored adults in the Northern Division in 1870 was 41.3, in 1880, 31.9; adult males, 1870, 38.6, 1880, 31.8; adult females, 1870, 44.1. 1880, 38.0.

In the Pacific Division the adult colored illiterates increased during the decade. Thus: in 1870 the adult colored illiterates were 15.7, in 1880, 33.2; adult males in 1870, 13.3, in 1880, 27.3; adult females in 1870, 33.1; 1880, 62.6. (In this Division of States the colored population doubled om 1870 to 1880.)

These figures, as to the Northern Division of States, as they concern both races, and as to the Pacific Division, as they concern the white race, are interesting, instructive and encouraging; they show that a thoroughly efficient common school makes appreciable gains on the enormous increments of illiteracy that immigration brings to these sections of the country.

A comparison of these tables for 1870 and 1880 will give us substantial encouragement as to the Southern Division of States also. While there was an absolute increase of adult illiteracy in the Southern Division, there was an appreciable and important relative decrease. The number of illiterate white adults in the Southern Division in 1870 was 820,257, or 19.4 per cent, in 1880, 965,389, or 16.6 per cent; of illiterate white voters there were in 1870, 318,495, or 15.1 per cent, in 1880, 411,900, or 14.3 per cent.

White women, in 1870, 501,762, or 23.7 per cent, in 1880, 553,489, or 19.4 per cent. (Even in the Northern and Western Divisions there was a slight absolute increase of adult illiteracy for both races. Thus: in the Northern Division in 1870 the adult white illiterates were 1,005,155, in 1880, 1,008,618; of adult colored illiterates there were in 1870, 74,281, in 1880, 91,746; in the Pacific Division the adult white illiterates numbered in 1870, 69,276, in 1880, 82,456; adult colored illiterates in 1870, 9,689; in 1880, 37,156.)

The comparison of these tables, all things considered, is very encouraging to the friends of the education of the colored people in the late slave States. In these States the adult colored illiterates numbered in 1870 1,736,538, or 88.9 per cent.; in 1880 2,018,998. or 78.9 per cent. The illiterate colored voters in the southern division numbered in 1870 828,212, or 87.8 per cent.; in 1880 951,944, or 76.0 per cent.; the illiterate colored women numbered in 1870 908,326, or 89.9 per cent.; in 1880 1,067,054, or 81.8 per cent.

But it will be misleading to trust very largely in the lowered per centage of illiteracy among the adult colored people. We must remember that many thousands of the older people, whose illiteracy antedated emancipation, died between 1870 and 1880. It is, perhaps, impossible to determine what has been gained; it is safe to believe that the efforts that have been made to educate the colored people have resulted in some real relative decrease in their illiteracy. It is certain that these efforts have at least prevented an enormous increase of illiteracy. We can hardly reach certainty in our estimates till the ante-bellum adult colored population has passed away. In the question we are considering that population is an unknown quantity.

A comparison of the statistics for 1870 and 1880 showing the illiteracy of persons "10 or more years old" will be instructive. Tables VII. and VIII. show that in each of the great divisions of States, and in nearly every State, there was a relative gain for intelligence among persons ten years old and upward. There was, as we have seen, in the Pacific Division, a gain of colored illiteracy. In the Northern Division the per centage of illiterate whites, ten years old and upward, in 1870, was 7.3; in 1880, 5 5; of colored illiterates in 1870, 35.5; in 1880, 29.2. In the Southern Division, illiterate whites in 1870, 21.91; in 1880, 18.9; colored in 1870, 85.2; in 1880, 75.0. In the Pacific Division, illiterate whites in 1870, 14.8; in 1880, 8.4; colored, 1870, 16.7; in 1880, 33.4.

There was an unwonted increase in the colored population in the Pacific division between 1870 and 1880.

SCHOOLS, TEACHERS AND PUPILS.

We will now consider more specifically the case of the *Negro at School*.

The following table, taken from the Report of the Commissioner of Education, General John Eaton, for 1883–84, gives a general view—shows the number of schools for the colored race and enrollment in them, by institutions, without reference to States, for 1882.

CLASS OF INSTITUTIONS.	Schools.	Enrolment.
Public Schools	15,932 *	802,982
Normal Schools	· 56	8,509
Institutions for Secondary Instruction	43	6,632
Universities and Colleges	18	2,298
Schools of Theology	24	665
Schools of Law	4	53
Schools of Medicine	3	125
Schools for the Deaf and Dumb and Blind	6	116
Total	16,086	821,380

* The Commissioner says in a foot note : "There should be added 391 schools, having an enrolment of 31,125 in reporting free States, making total number of colored public schools 16,323 and total enrolment in them 834,107. This makes the total number of schools, as far as reported, 16,477, and total number of the colored race under instruction in them 852,505. The colored public schools in those States in which no separate reports are made, however, are not included."

The following tables give an instructive summary of statistics of institutions for the instruction of the colored race, by States, for 1882 :

States and Territories.	Public Schools.		Normal Schools.			Institutions for secondary instruction.		
	School population.	Enrolment.	Schools.	Teachers.	Pupils.	Schools.	Teachers.	Pupils.
Alabama	176,533	69,479	7	31	1,050	4	20	611
Arkansas	69,113	23,139	2	11	429	2		
Delaware	4,152	2,544						
Florida	47,583	27,012				2	10	313
Georgia	234,889	95,055	3	7	441	7	25	1,181
Kansas						1		
Kentucky	94,678	20,223	1	8	317	1	9	192
Louisiana	142,190	23,500	3	5	95	2	6	255
Maryland	74,192	29,931	2	10	246	1		60
Mississippi	253 212	125,633	3	22	485	1	2	100
Missouri	41,790	24,838	1	6	143			
North Carolina	176,836	88,236	9	32	898	3	15	375
Ohio			1	1	7	1	3	60
Pennsylvania			1	7	257			
South Carolina	167,829	80,575	5	28	1,061	6	40	1,722
Tennessee	140,815	56,676	8	49	1,691	1	2	75
Texas	57,510	37,781	2	6	50	7	19	962
Virginia	240,950	85,328	4	62	820	3	13	658
West Virginia	8,420	4,416	1	8	230			
District of Columbia.	13,915	9,593	3	14	284			
Indian Territory						1	3	68
Total	1,944,572	802,982	56	307	8,509	43	167	6,632

States and Territories.	Universities and colleges.			Schools of Theology.			Schools of Law.		
	Schools.	Teachers.	Pupils.	Schools.	Teachers.	Pupils.	Schools.	Teachers.	Pupils.
Alabama.............	.....	.....	.....	3	5	89	.....	.....	.....
Arkansas.............	.....	.....	.....	.....	.....	.....	.....	.....	.....
Delaware.............	.....	.....	.....	.....	...	.....	...	.....	.....
Florida..	.....	.....	.....	.....	...	.....	.....	.....	.....
Georgia.............	2	24	60	1	.....	.....	.....	.....	.....
Kansas.............	.....	.....	.....	.....	.....	.....	.....	.....	.....
Kentucky	1	9	104	1	9	10	.....	.....	.....
Louisiana.............	3	14	345	3	5	65	1	4	20
Maryland	.....	.....	.....	1	4	30	.....	.....	.....
Mississippi.............	2	12	526	1	5	30	.....	.....	.....
Missouri...	.....	.....	.....	.....	.....	.....	.....	.....	.....
North Carolina....	2	21	806	2	8	106	.....	.....	.....
Ohio..	1	7	171	1	...	.....	.....	.....	.....
Pennsylvania	1	.....	182	1	5	14	.....	.....	.....
South Carolina.........	2	23	294	3	8	33	1	3	8
Tennessee	2	17	273	3	17	137	1	5	.....
Texas	.....	.....	.....	1	1	13	.....	.....	.....
Virginia.............	1	.....	.....	1	5	63	.....	.....	.....
West Virginia....	.....	.....	.....	...	...	.....	.....	.....	.....
District of Columbia....	1	6	47	2	7	75	1	4	20
Indian Territory....	.....	.....	.....	.....	.....	.....	.....	.....	.....
Total.	18	133	2,208	24	79	665	4	16	55

States and Territories.	Schools of medicine.			Schools for the deaf and dumb and the blind.		
	Schools.	Teachers.	Pupils.	Schools.	Teachers.	Pupils.
Georgia.........................	.....	.....	.....	2	.....	2
Maryland	.....	.....	.....	1	5	32
Mississippi	.....	.....	.....	1	.....	14
North Carolina.................	1	1	3	1	15	60
Tennessee.	1	13	29	1	.....	8
District of Columbia.	1	9	93	.....	.....	.....
Total.......................	3	23	125	6	20	116

The following table gives the comparative statistics of education in the Southern States :

Table showing comparative school population and enrolment of the white and colored races in the public schools of the recent slave States, with total expenditure for the same in 1882.

States.	White.			Colored.			Total expenditure for both races. a
	School population.	Enrolment.	Percentage of the school population enrolled.	School population.	Enrolment.	Percentage of the school population enrolled.	
Alabama	224,461	107,949	48	176,538	69,479	39	$ 403,602
Arkansas............	b212,940	b76,598	36	b69,113	b23,139	33	5 43,857
Delaware...........	c33,133	c26,578	c80	c1,152	c2,544	c61	d207,231
Florida.............	c19,641	f24,933	50	c47,583	f27,012	57	133,260
Georgia	g261,884	161,377	62	g234,689	95,055	40	584,174
Kentucky	c177,215	c236,440	c50	h94,578	i20,223	d21	j1,248,524
Louisiana	c123,224	c35,870	c30	c142,190	c23,500	c17	c441,481
Maryland.	c246,009	131,011	53	c74,192	28,034	39	1,651,908
Mississippi...........	f190,919	c111,655	58	f253,212	c125,633	50	c757,758
Missouri	706,850	467,911	66	41,790	k24,833	59	3 753,234
North Carolina......	236,324	144,835	51	176,236	88,236	50	1509,736
South Carolina	c94 450	65,399	69	c167,829	80,575	48	378,886
Tennessee...........	408,361	207,680	51	140,818	56,676	40	827,154
Texas....	b173,942	105,179	60	b57,510	37,731	66	803,850
Virginia	311,827	172 034	55	240,989	85,328	35	1,157,142
West Virginia	208,178	151,098	73	8,420	4,446	53	879,820
District of Columbia	c29,592	c17,716	60	c43,945	c9,583	69	579,312
Total	4,016,956	2,249,263	.....	1,944,572	802,952	......	14,820,972

a In Delaware, in addition to the school tax collected from colored citizens, which has heretofore been the only State appropriation for the support of colored schools, the legislature now appropriates annually $2,400 from the State treasury for educating the colored children of the State ; in Maryland, there is a biennial appropriation ; in the District of Columbia, one-third of the school funds is set apart for colored public schools ; in South Carolina, the school moneys are distributed in proportion to the average attendance, without regard to race ; and in other States mentioned above, the school moneys are divided in proportion to the school population, without regard to race.
b As far as reported ; several counties failed to make race distinctions.
c In 1881.
d In 1880.
e United States Census of 1880.
f Estimated.
g Four counties failing to report.
h Number of colored children in Kentucky between the ages of 6 and 20 according to the United States Census of 1880 ; in 1882 the school age for colored children was changed by law from 6-16 to 6-20.
i According to return for 1880 ; since then the legal school age for colored children has been lengthened by four years.
j For 1881 ; in 1882 the per capita of the white child of legal school age and the colored child of legal school age was made the same, thus giving to the colored children equal advantages with the white children in the common school fund of the State.
k Thirty-two counties failing to report.
l Fifteen counties failing to report.

These tables give us for 1882 in the Southern States, a total school population of 5,991,528. (The school age in these States averages from six to nineteen years.) Of the whole number 4,046,956 were white; 1,944,572 were colored children. Of the white children 2 249,263 were enrolled; of the colored 802,982, that is something more than half the white children, and something less than half the colored children were enrolled. To state it otherwise, of the white school population 56.0 per cent. were at school; of the colored 45.70 per cent. There is reason to believe that not less than 300,000 white children were in private schools; only a small proportion of colored children were in private schools. Counting public and private schools, about five-eighths of the white children, and possibly one-half the colored children were at school.

A comparison of the reports of the Commissioner of Education for 1880, 1881 and 1882, will show a decrease in the number of schools for colored children in the Southern States. The total number for 1880 was 16,800, for 1881, 17,248; for 1882, 15,932. These figures do not prove decreased attendance; the actual enrolment was largest in 1882. The enrollment in the public schools for 1880 was 784,709; for 1881, 802,559; for 1882, 802,982. In the Southern States the school funds are disbursed without distinction of race, except as indicated in note (*a*), page 11.

What is the quality of these public schools for colored children ?

Those who approve only the best schools will condemn these. They are not to be compared with the best public schools in the country; it would be unjust to all parties concerned in them to judge them by the highest examples. We should consider that twenty years ago there were no public or other schools for these people. These schools are in every respect better than the majority of men esteemed as reasonable expected, when the experiment began, to see in twice twenty years.

The school term is short, running from three to five months; the average colored school in the Southern States is not open more than three months in the year. In the country districts the white public schools are not open for a longer period. The "average duration of public schools in days" in the United States, not counting the territories, is 119.63 days; in the Southern States 100.3. As the school term in Maryland and Delaware is above the average of the whole country, being in Maryland 199 and in Delaware 153 days, this statement would be misleading. Take Alabama, Georgia, Louisiana, Mississippi, North Carolina, South Carolina, Texas and Virginia, and the average length of the public school year is 81.6 days.

Most of the school buildings in the rural districts are inferior; the schools for the colored people in the rural districts and in the small villages are, as a rule, held in the church buildings of the colored people, and these are, generally speaking, better than the white people's public school buildings, and are located to suit the convenience of those who use them. The appliances are few and simple; the primary texts necessary in teaching the elements; cheap globes and charts are occasionally seen; they are generally given by some friend; they do not characterize the system. Neither is the use of these and other such appliances common in the public schools for the whites. The texts used in the public schools of the Southern States by the children of both races, are those that are issued by the great Northern publishers, and are such as have the approval of experts and eminent authorities. The exceptions to this statement are so small as to be unappreciable.

Most important of all in an inquiry of this sort is the quality and character of the teachers themselves. The tenth census shows that there were in the United States in 1880, 16,800 "separate schools for colored children;" it also shows that there were 15,834 colored teachers. Of the schools reported for colored children in 1880 16,418 were in the Southern States; of the colored teachers 15,488 were in the Southern States. These figures do not mean that in 1880 nearly 1000 colored public schools in the Southern States were taught by white people, but that many colored teachers were left out of the enumeration. The figures mean that, considered as a system, colored teachers teach the colored schools. The tendency to this adjustment is not peculiar to the Southern States; outside the late slave States there were, in 1880, 382 separate schools for colored children, and 346 colored teachers.

The history of education among the colored people during the last twenty years, and all the facts now observable, lead to the certain conclusion that common schools for colored children must depend on colored teachers.

It may be remarked, that nearly two-thirds of these colored teachers are men. Thus: the census shows in 1880 10,520 colored men, and 5,314 colored women engaged in the public schools.

Many of the teachers in the colored public schools are pitiably incompetent—the statement need not be qualified by the word "colored" if we were considering the whole case of the public schools in the Southern States. Many of them lack not only scholarship and training, but moral character. As a rule, there is good reason to believe that they do the best they can; not a few of them do admirably well; some do their work so efficiently and usefully as to justify the belief that the colored people are capable of furnishing fit material for making teachers of the most approved quality. The defects of these colored teachers are so great as to create an urgent necessity for training better ones; their excellencies and their successes are sufficient to justify the best hopes of success in the effort, and to vindicate the judgment of those who make large investments of money and service to give to colored students opportunity of thoroughly preparing themselves for the work of teaching the children of their people.

This Board of Trust comes into relations with the work of educating the colored people through its connection with those training schools where, if anywhere, for years to come, young men and women are to get ready to teach. There is, perhaps, not one inquiry of greater importance that this Board can raise than the question of the character of the schools in the South that propose to provide for the higher instruction of the colored people. For out of these schools the teachers come, and they will determine the educational destiny of the generation they teach or mislead.

Counting all the higher grade schools, not including professional schools, the report of the Commissioner for 1882-3 shows a total of 117, counting those called normal schools, institutes, seminaries, colleges and universities. Most of these institutions have been established and carried on by churches and benevolent associations—northern people furnishing nearly all the money. A few of them have been established by the States in which they are placed, and are sustained by public money.

In these higher grade schools there were in 1882, according to the Commissioner's report, 607 teachers, the majority being women. In the schools to which appropriations were made from the "John F. Slater Fund" during the school year 1883-84 there were employed that year 303 teachers.

What sort of men and women are they who are engaged in the higher grade schools for colored youth in the Southern States? As a rule there are no teachers in this country more competent or faithful, and no missionaries in any country more consecrated to Christian work. The foremost training schools, colleges and universities in the United States are represented in these teachers. There is reason for saying with confidence that, with few exceptions, these men and women could get better pay elsewhere; they are in these colored schools because they feel called of God to do this work. Your Agent has found cultured young women working enthusiastically and efficiently for $15 a month and board. In one of the schools, a school approved on all hands, the lady principal, a graduate of Mt. Holyoke, was working at $25 per month and board. This she had been doing for fifteen years. She is a woman of rare quality, as your Agent found while she was a guest at his house in Oxford, Ga., and while he was a guest in her school in ——. The pay of these teachers will not average $50 per month.

They are people of most uncommon energy and industry; theirs is a hard service and many of them, after a few years, are worn out by the labors they perform.

In the schools to which appropriations have been made
from the "John F. Slater Fund" are teachers from Wesleyan University (Middletown, Conn.), Wellesley Smith, University of Michigan, Baldwin University, Colby University, Yale, Amherst, Dartmouth, University of Boston,
Union College, Rutgers, Vassar, Mt. Holyoke, Baker University (Kansas), Vanderbilt University (Nashville,Tenn.).
Western Reserve College (Ohio), Ohio Wesleyan, Madison
University, Olivet (Michigan), Aberdeen(Scotland), various
normal schools of high degree in Massachusetts, Pennsyl-
vania, New York, Maine, Ohio and other training schools
of the first grade.

It is particularly worthy of mention that among the teachers engaged in these southern training schools for colored
teachers are a number of colored men and women who have
successfully prepared themselves for their work at the older
and better schools established for their people in the South.
Among these teachers are graduates of Hampton Institute,
the Atlanta University, Fisk, Howard University and
others.

The success of these colored principals and professors
demonstrates the capacity of colored students to become
the efficient leaders of education among their people when
time and opportunity have enabled them to show what
they can do. This is most important; for if it were proved
that the race could not furnish its own educators it would be
proved that the race never could be educated. But it has
been proved that the negro race in the Southern States is
capable of furnishing its own teachers. It is necessary, if
this great movement to educate and Christianize these people is to succeed, if it is to be saved from total collapse, that
the white people should, for a long time, not only furnish
most of the money required to carry on the work, but most
of the men and women who are to give it direction. The
white people can continue in this work all the more hope-
fully when they see that a few of the colored race, taught and
trained in these schools,show capacity for educational leadership. That not a few colored people feel themselves capable of
leadership, and evince undue eagerness (their instinct for

seeking leadership is strong) to assume its burdens and responsibilities will require patience, firmness and wisdom in those who have been the best friends and most efficient helpers these people ever had.

Most of the higher grade schools for colored people are wisely located, and they are fairly distributed through the Southern States.

The financial management of the societies that have been engaged in this work has been exceptionally able. As a rule, they have rigidly avoided debt; during the twenty years they have been founding and conducting schools for the colored people, no important enterprise has fallen through by financial failure. The Rev. Dr. R. S. Rust, Secretary of the Freedmen's Aid Society, in his official report for 1881, made the following statement: "Fully $300,000 have been invested in permanent real estate, lands and buildings, on which there is not a dollar of indebtedness." Substantially this statement applies to the investments of the other great societies.

Their projectors and friends have sometimes been mildly censured for giving to some of these institutions names too large for them. It is an ungrateful task to find fault with people who mean so well, and work so efficiently. When these institutions have grown to be what their names signify, the occasion for criticism will have passed away. Some day some of them will come into this fullness and maturity of development.

That some evil, incidental to the overnaming alluded to, has followed, is obvious. A few of these evils a friend may indicate without the need of amplification. To not a few colored people the over-large names have been misleading. Having attended ———— University for a time, it is not unnatural for an imperfectly trained student to conclude that he has a University education, and is entitled to the consideration which his supposed attainments deserve. Colored churches that have embarked in the work of founding schools, have promptly imitated the example set them by their white friends, and have named schools of inferior grade and small resources, Universities. Many things they must learn and unlearn on these subjects by experience.

2

The great names have been occasions of prejudice among
many Southern and not a few Northern people, against the
whole work of education among the colored people. As-
suming that ―――― University is really attempting university work, some have ridiculed the whole business and
others have called in question the wisdom of the effort,
when there is so great and universal need of elementary
education. Not a few would have helped the work that is
really being done if they had not been under the impres-
sion that something very different is being attempted.

WHAT THESE SCHOOLS ARE DOING.

It is always best to know what the facts are when an
opinion is to be reached as to the merits of a question in
discussion, or as to the methods to be adopted in order to
accomplish desired results. That the Board of Trustees of
the John F. Slater Fund, and others, who may read this
paper, may have full opportunity to consider and understand the character and methods of the higher grade schools
for colored people in the Southern States, it is thought best
to introduce here very full illustrative statements concern-
ing what is really proposed and what is really done by a
number of representatative Southern schools for colored
youths.

FISK UNIVERSITY, Nashville, Tenn., may be taken as a fair
illustration of the work done by some of the more advanced
of these schools. In its course of study, as well as in the
merit of its work, it is doubtful if there is one that goes
beyond it.

This institution was organized in 1865, under the auspices of the American Missionary Association. It has been
under rarely competent management, and its success has
been great. Its "Jubilee singers" have made its name familiar to two continents. Its real estate and improvements are
worth fully $300,000, and, while it lacks much that it needs
and deserves, its equipments are every way superior to
those of a majority of the better class of these institutions.
The annual catalogue for 1884 shows twenty officers and

teachers, and 442 pupils. From this catalogue the names and positions of the faculty, the courses of study, and the summary of attendance are taken, in order to illustrate the character of the work done by Fisk University.

OFFICERS AND INSTRUCTORS —Rev. E. M. Cravath, M. A., President, and Professor of Mental and Moral Science; Rev. A. K. Spence, M. A., Dean of the Faculty, and Professor of Greek and French; Rev. H. S. Bennett, M. A., Professor of Theology and German, and University Pastor; Miss Helen C. Morgan, M. A., Professor of Latin; Rev. F. A. Chase, M. A., Professor of Natural Science; Herbert H. Wright, M. A., Professor of Mathematics and Vocal Music; Miss Harriet Cushman, M. A., Principal of the Young Lad es' Department; Mrs. Liva A. Shaw, Instructor in Normal Department; Miss Henrietta Matson, Principal of Common English Department; Mrs. Abbie A Sprague, Instructor in English Grammar and Composition; Miss Mary E. Edwards, Instructor in Arithmetic, Penmanship and Drawing; Miss Hattie M. Curtis, Instructor in Geography and United States H story; Miss M. A. Perry, in charge of Intermediate School; Miss Mary A. Dwight, in charge of the Model School and Practice Teaching; Rev. C. W Hawley, M. A., Treasurer; Miss Anna Whelan, instructor in Instrumental and Vocal Music; Miss Juliet B. Smith, instructor in Nursing and charge of Health Department; Miss Melissa Ritter, instructor in Cooking and Sewing; Miss L. A. Parmelee, Matron of Livingston Hall; Miss Fanny Gleason, Matron of Jubilee Hall.

COURSES OF STUDY.

The following courses of study have been es ablished. D partments of Law and Medicine will be added as demanded by the best interests of the University.

COLLEGE DEPARTMENT.

For admission to this department, the candidate must have passed through the College Preparatory Course of Study, or its equiva ent. Upon completing the course, the student is graduated with the degree of Bachelor of Arts. Students omitting either the Latin or Greek of the College Course, and pursuing, instead, such other studies as the Faculty may direct, are, graduated with the degree of Bachelor of Science.

Freshman Year—First Term —Latin: Virgil's Æneid (Chase and Stuart). Greek—Anabasis and Greek Testament. Mathematics—University Algebra (Davies') Completed; Geometry (Peck).

Second Term.—Latin—Cicero, De Senectute and Latin Prose Composition Chase and Stuart). Greek—Xenophon's Memorabilia and Plato's Phædo (Boise and Freeman). Mathematics—Geometry Completed; Trigonometry Completed (Peck); Surveying (Murray).

Sophomore Year—First Term.—Greek—Homer's Iliad (Boise), or Odyssey (Boise and Freeman). Mathematics—Conic Sections (Peck); Calculus, optional. Rhetoric—Reed and Kellogg. French—Grammar, Exercises and Translations.

Second Term.—Latin—Horace's Odes and Satires (Chase and Stewart); Roman History. Mathematics—Calculus, optional. French—Trans'ation; Study of French Literature. Physical Science—Botany (Wood). Herbarium, with fifty specimes, required.

Junior Year—First Term.—Latin—Livy (Chase and Stewart); Tacitus (Tyler). Physical Science –Physics (Norton). German—Grammar, Exercises and Translations (Worman).

Second Term.—Greek: Demosthenes' Oration on the Crown (D'Ooge), and Antigone of Sophocles. Physical Science : Physiology and Hygiene (Martin); Astronomy (Lockyer). German : Worman.

Senior Year—First Term.—Mental Science : Hopkin's Outline Study of Man. English Literature : Shaw. Logic : McCosh. Physical Science : Chemistry (Elliott & Storer's Elemen's), with practice in Laboratory.

Second Term.—Moral Science: Fairchild's Moral Philosophy. Logic : McCosh. Constitutional Law : Andrews Manual of the Constitution of the United States. Political Economy : Wayland (Chapin.) Physical Science : Zoology (Tenney); Geology and Mineralogy (Dana), with field work and blow-pipe determina ions. Weekly Exercises in Declamations, Essays and original Addresses, during the entire course.

COLLEGE PREPARATORY DEPARTMENT.

For admission to this depa tment, the candidate must have completed the studies of the Common English Department, or their equivalent. On completing this course, the student is admitted to the College Department.

Junior Year—First Term —Latin : Harkness' Intrcductory Book. Geology of Tennessee Agriculture and Elementary Science. Mathematics : Elementary Algebra.

Second Term.—Latin · Harkness' Introductory Book, Grammar and Reader. Book-keeping: Bryant and Stratton. History : Anderson's General History. Mathemat cs : Elementary Algebra.

Middle Class—First Term.—Latin: Harkness' Cæsar. Greek : Hadley's Grammar; Boise's First Lessons through Declension. Mathematics : Higher Arithmetic (Davies').

Second Term.—Latin : Harkness' Cæsar and Cicero's Orations (Chase and Stuart). Greek. Grammar, continued ; First Lessons completed. Mathematics : Higher Arithmetic.

Senior Class—First Term.—Latin : Cicero's Ora ions (Chase and Stuart). Greek : Xenophon's Anabasis (Boise); Greek Testament. Mathematics : University Algebra (Davies').

Second Term. –Latin : Virgil's Eneid (Chase and Stuart). Greek : Pro e Composition (Jones). Mathematics : Manual of Geome ry) Peck). Rhetorical Exe:cises weekly during the course.

THEOLOGICAL DEPARTMENT.

Theological instruction is given to young men who desire to prepare themselves for the ministry, either in connection with their other studies or after these are completed.

The advantages of this department are open to persons of all Christian denominations. Students having the ministry immediately in view are admitted to instruction in other departments without paying tuition. In cases of need, additional aid can frequently be given by special arrangement, previously made. The course of instruction in Theology is to be enlarged and made to constitute a distinct department as soon as practicable.

First Year.—Biblical Exegesis, Skeletonizing, Sermonizing Lectures on Homiletics and on Mental and Moral Philosophy, Rhetorical Exercises.

Second Year.—Biblical Exegesis, Sermonizing. Systematic Theology (Pond), Biblical Geography, Rules of Interpretation, Rhetorical Exercises.

Third Year.—Topical Exegesis, Ecclesiastical History (Guericke), Biblical Archæology, Lectures on Pastoral Theology, Sermonizing. In addition to this, instruction will be given, if thought best, in the original languages of the Scriptures.

NORMAL DEPARTMENT.

For admission to this department the candidate must have completed the studies of the Common English Department, or their equivalent.

Elementary Course, First Year.—Elementary Algebra, Grammar and Composition, Commercial Geography (one term), Physical Geography (Guyot), Drawing Morals and Manners (Gow), Latin, Music.

Second Year.—Higher Arithmetic and Book-keeping, Physiology, Botany (one term), Literature, (Seven British Classics or equivalent), School Economy and Primary Methods, Latin, Drawing, Music.

Students who complete this course receive a certificate of their fitness to teach in Public Schools.

Advanced Course, Junior.—Plane Geometry, Physics, General History, Scripture History, (New Testament), English Literature (Gilman), Drawing, Practice Teaching.

Seniors.—Astronomy (Lockyer), Geology, Mental and Moral Philosophy, United States History and Civil Government, Pedagogics, Review of Common Branches, Practice Teaching.

Students who complete this Advanced Normal Course are graduated from the Normal Department and given a diploma. The special object of this course of study is to properly qualify persons for teaching in advanced grades.

COMMON ENGLISH DEPARTMENT.

For the present this department seems a necessity in order to meet the wants of the people in whose interest this University has been especially founded. It provides for a thorough and systematic course of study in the common branches, and lays a good foundation in correct habits of study for the advanced courses. In order to be admitted to this department, the pupil must pass a satisfactory examination in the Third Reader, Intermediate Arithmetic through fractions, and Primary Geography.

Class D.—Fourth Reader, Intermediate Arithmetic, completed, Comprehensive Geography begun (U. S. and N. A.), Language Lessons (Knox or Powell), Spelling, Copy Books (Nos. 3 and 4) Drawing, Vocal Music.

Class C.—Fifth Reader, Practical Arithmetic through fractions, Geography of South America and Europe, Elementary Grammar, (Reed or Kellogg), Familiar Science, Writing, Drawing, Vocal Music.

Class B.—Fifth Reader, Practical Arithmetic through percentage, Geography completed, Grammar, Mental Arithmetic, Writing, Drawing, Vocal Music.

Class A.—Practical Arithmetic completed, Grammar and Composition, U. S. History (Barnes or Higginson's), Alcohol and Hygiene (Coleman), Reading and Writing, Drawing, Vocal Music.

THE MODEL SCHOOL.

This is designed especially as a school of observation and practice in connection with the Normal Department. The course of study covers the first four years of a graded course, and a limited number of pupils are admitted.

MUSIC.

Much attention is paid to Music, both instrumental and vocal, including Vocal Culture. Instruction is given on both Piano and Organ For terms see *Expenses.* Vocal music is taught free of charge.

What are these four hundred and forty-two students doing? Not what one familiar only with the work of really first-class institutions, bearing the title of college or university, for white students might suppose, but *just what they ought to be doing.* Here follows the official statement of the classification of the students.

SUMMARY.

College Department.	Male.	Female.	Total
Seniors	4	0	4
Juniors	12	4	16
Sophomores	4	0	4
Freshmen	6	3	9—33
College Preparatory Department.			
Senior Preparatory	7	6	13
Middle Preparatory	15	5	20
Junior Preparatory	13	2	15—48
Theological Department.			
	10	0	10—10
Normal Department			
Seniors	3	2	5
Juniors	0	3	3
Second Year	4	8	12
First Year	5	4	9—29

Common English Department.	Male.	Female.	Total.
Class A	18	14	32
Class B	26	20	46
Class C	33	24	57
Class D	30	41	71-206
Intermediate School	22	39	61—61
Model School	27	38	65—65
Pupils in Instrumental Music	7	50	57—57
Total in all departments			509
Counted more than once			67
Totals : males, 229; femal s, 213			412
Boarders : males, 135; females, 114			249

The first alumni are of the class of 1875. From 1875 to 1883, the alumni number 32. It will be interesting and instructive to give the entire list; it will show how few complete the advanced course, and it will indicate what such exceptionally successful students do after leaving the university.

ALUMNI.

Class 1875.—Jas D. Burrus, M. A., professor in Alcorn University, Rodney, Miss ; John H. Burrus, M. A. president Alcorn University, Rodney, Miss.; America W. Rob nson, (Lucas) B. A. teacher, Macon, Miss.; Virginia, E Walker (Broughton) M. A., teacher, Memphis, Tenn.

Class 1877.—Laura S. Cary,* B. A., late instructor in Fisk University; Young A. Wallace, B S teacher, Florence, Ala.

Class 1878.—Henry S. Merry, B. A., principal of Colored Schools, Clarksville Tenn.; Albert P. Mi ler, B. A., theological student, Yale College, New Haven, Ct.

Class 1879.—Preston R Burrus, B A., principal city school, Nashville, Tenn.; Jennie H. K. H bbs, B. A. teacher, Nashvil e, Tenn.; Austin J. Merry, B A., principal col red school, Jackson, Tenn.; Lulu F. Parker, B. S, teacher, Memphis, Tenn.

Class 1880.—Ernest H Anderson, B. A., princip l State Normal School, Hempstead, Texas; Laurine C. Ande son, B. A., teacher State Normal School, Hempstead, Tex.; Joseph Anderson, B. A., teacher, Leesburg, Tex; Jacob J. Durham, B. A., minister, Columbia, S. C.; Robert P. Neal, B. A., t acher, Humboldt, Tenn.; John E. Porter, B. A., principal colored Hig School, Jeffersonville, Ind.

Class 1881.—David N Crosthwait, B. A., teacher, Nashville, Tenn.; William H. Hodgkins, B. A., lawyer, N shville, Tenn.; George W. Moore, B A., minister Washington, D. C.; Benj F Ousley, Jr., B. A., theological student, Oberlin, Ohio; Albert M. Thomas, Jr., B. A., law

*Deceased June 27, 1879.

student, Yale College, New Haven, Ct.; John M. Turpin, B. A., teacher, Columbia, Tenn.

Class 1882.—Wiiliam D. Donnell, B. A., principal colored school, Topeka, Kansas.

Class 1883.—Henrietta Bailey. B. A.. teacher, Corinth. Miss.; Henry C. Gray, B. A., theological s ndent. Ober in, Ohio ; Humphrev L Jones, B. A., teacher, Richmond, Texas; John C. McAdams, B. A., principal colored school, Shelbyville. Tenn.; Samuel A. Mc Alwee, B. A., member of Tennessee Legislature, Brownsville. Tenn ; Nelson T. Mitch-ll, B. A., principal colored school, Sparta, Ill.; Tolbert F. Sublett, B. A., tutor in Alcorn University, Rodney, Miss.

The CENTRAL TENNESSEE College, Nashville, Tenn., furnishes another example of admirable work, and is fairly illustrative of the best among the institutions for colored people called "colleges."

This institution was inaugurated in 1866 under the auspices of the "Freedmen's Aid Society" of the Methodist Episcopal Church. Its investments in real estate and improvements are worth about $100.000. The catalogue shows, in addition to the regular college departments, three professional schools—a School of Law, a School of Medicine, and a School of Theology. The College department has a faculty of fifteen and 360 students; the law department has a faculty of five with two students, both juniors in 1884; the medical department has a faculty of ten with 31 students, Seniors 8, juniors 23.* The theological department has a faculty of three with 30 students. Most of the theological students are also in the college department.

The names and positions of the regular faculty are copied from the catalogue.

FACULTY.—Rev. H. M Tupper, A. M., President, Professor of Systematic Theology ; F. A. Spafford, M. D., Professor of Anat my and Natu a! Science ; F. W. Perry. Professor of Latin and Greek; Rev N. F. Roberts. A. M., Associate Professor of Mathematics and B blical Studies; Rev. J. S. Lea, A. B., Professor in Normal and Classical Department; Rev. E. H. Lipscombe, A. M., Professor of Rhetoric and Moral Philosophy ; Erasmus

*The Medical Department of this institution is "Meharry Medi al College." The commodious four-story brick building is the gif of the Meharry brothers. The on struction in this department is thorough. In addition to the work done by the regular faculty of ten competent physicians several of the profe -ors of the Medic l De artment of Vanderbilt University and of the Medical Department of the University of Tennessee deliver occasional lectures, as the Dean of the Faculty, G. W. Hubbard, M D., informs us in the annual announcement.

K. Bradway, Instructor in Mechanical Department; Mrs. F. W. Perry, Teacher in Mathematics and in charge of Model School; Miss Belle Pettigrew, Missionary and Instructor in Hygiene—Female Department; Mrs. F. A. Spafford, Instructor in Music and Free-hand Drawing; Miss Lizzie Porter, Instructor in Dress-Making and Domestic Arts; Mrs E. K. Bradway, Assistant Instructor in Sewing and Dress-Making.

Lectures on Biblical topics have been given during the year by Rev. Dr. Skinner, Pastor of First Baptist Church, (white) and Rev. Mr. Gwaltney, Pastor of Second Baptist Church (white).

The entire course of studies in the literary departments is presented here :

STUDIES.

COLLEGIATE CLASSES—FRESHMAN YEAR

First Term.—Geometry, Cicero's Orations, Latin Composition, Xenophon's Memorabilia, Rhetoric.

Second Term.—Geometry, Livy, Homer's Iliad, Greek Composition, Rhetoric.

Third Term.—Algebra Completed, Livy and Horace, Herodotus, Botany.

SOPHOMORE YEAR.

First Term.—Trigonometry and Mensuration, Horace's Odes and Epistles, Demosthenes, Chemistry.

Second Term.—Surveying, with field work, De Senectute and De Amicitia, Thucydides, Chemistry, laboratory work.

Third Term.—Analytical Geometry, Tacitus, Plato, Geology.

JUNIOR YEAR.

First Term.—Olmstead's Mechanical Philosophy, Quintillian, Greek, New Testament Gospels, Evidences of Christianity.

Second Term.—Olmstead's Mechanical and Natural Philosophy, Greek, Epistles of St. Paul or Hebrews, Moral Science, Microscopy.

Third Term.—Mathematical Astronomy, Greek or Hebrew, English Language and Literature, Political Economy.

SENIOR YEAR.

First Term.—Differential Calculus, History of Philosophy, Chemical Analysis, laboratory work twice a week.

Second Term.—Integral Calculus, Superhuman Origin of the Bible, Rogers: Logic, Mineralogy, laboratory work twice a week.

Third Term.—Butler's Analogy Mental Science, Thesis on some part of the course of study for graduating address. Review and examination on common English branches including Arithmetic, Grammar. Geography, History of the United States and English Literature. Students taking the Scientific Course will be required to take additional work in the laboratory, and one recitation in the ancient or modern languages. French or German may be substituted, by the consent of the Faculty, for one of the ancient languages, after the Freshman year.

PREPARATORY.

FIRST YEAR.

F rst Term.—Algebra. Lat'n, Harkness' Grammar and R ader, Ancient History and Geography.

Second Term.—Algebra, Latin, Harkness' Grammar and Reader, Mediæval and Modern H story.

Third Term.—A'gebra, Latin, Grammar and Reader, Mythology.

SECOND YEAR.

First Term.—Algebra, Latin, Cæsar's Commentary: Greek, Goodwin's Grammar, Greek Reader, English Language and Literature.

Second Term —Algebra, Latin. Cæsar's Co nmentary; Greek, Goodwin's Grammar, Greek Reader; English Language and Li erature.

Third Term.—Algebra, Latin. Cæsar's Co nmentary; Greek, Goodwin's Grammar, Greek Reade ; English Classics.

THIRD YEAR.

First Term.—Geometry, V rgil, An bysis Eng'ish History.

Second Term.—Geometry, Virgil, Anabasis, English History.

Third Term.—Geometry, Sallust. Anabasis, Astronomy, Amer can History.

Text Books.—Harkness' Latin and Goodwin's Greek Grammar; Anderson's Ancient History; Ray's Second Part Algebra; Steele's Natural Philosophy; Wentworth's Geometry; Davies' Trigonometry and Analytical Geometry and Calculus; Hanson an I Rolfe's Latin Prose and Poetical Selections; Leighton's Greek Selections, S eele's Chemistry; Wood's Botany; Tenny's Geology; History of Philosophy; Harper's Library; Dana's Mineralogy.

ACADEMIC.

First and Second years' studies t e ame as the Preparatory.

THIRD YEAR.

Fi st Term.—Geometry, Virgil, Anabasis Greek Composition, Rhetoric.

Second Term —Geometry. V rgil Anabasis, Rhetoric.

Third Term —Geometry, Anabasis, A-tronomy, Botany.

FOURTH YEAR.

First Term.—History of Philosophy, Evidences of Christianity, Chemistry.

Second Term —Chemistry work in laboratory, Mo al Science, Logic.

Third Term.—Review of English S udies, Butler's Analogy, Mental Science.

Studen s entering the Preparatory or Academic Courses will be required to pass a satisfactory ex mination on the Normal Course, or its equivalent.

NORMAL.

First year's studies same as first year's English Course.

First Term —Arithmetic, Denominate Numbers to Proportion; Geography, with map drawing, Grammar and Composition, History of the United States.

Second Term —Arithmetic to Interest, Geography, Grammar and Composition, Theory and Practice of Teaching History of the United States.

Third Term.—Arithmetic to Partnership, Grammar and Composition, School Government. Elements of Moral Science.

THIRD YEAR.

First Term —Arithmetic to Metric System; Physiology; Methods of Teaching, English Language and Literature.

Second Term —Arithmetic Completed and Reviewed, Civil Government, Natural History, School Laws, Rolls and Report of Teacher, English Language and Literature.

Third Term —Algebra Natural Philosophy Geology of Tennessee, Elements of Mental and Moral Science, School Management, Legal Responsibilities of Teachers, English Classics. Candidates for this course must pass examination on the fundamental rules of Arithmetic, and on the elements of other common English studies.

ENGLISH AND BUSINESS.

FIRST YEAR.

First Term —Fourth or Fifth Reader; Writing ; Spelling; Arithmetic from United States Money to Reduction of Fractions, Geography, Grammar, First Lessons.

Second Term.—Reading Writing, Spelling; Arithmetic to Abbreviated Processes; Grammar, First Lessons; Geography, Drawing.

Third Term.—Reading, Writing, Spelling; Arithmetic to Denominate Numbers; Geography, Grammar First Lessons; Drawing

SECOND YEAR.

First Term.—Reading, Arithmetic to Proportion, Grammar, Higher Lessons, History of the United States, Drawing.

Second Term.—Reading, Arithmetic to Interest; History of the United States; Grammar, Higher Lessons.

Third Term.— Arithmetic to Partnership; History of the United States; Grammar, Physiology.

THIRD YEAR

First Term. —Arithmetic to Metric System; Book-keeping; Natural History; Laws of Business.

Second Term.—Arithmetic Completed and Reviewed; Book-keeping; Civil Government; Legal Forms.

Third Term. —Business Arithmetic; Natural Philosophy; Book-keeping; Legal Forms, Reviews, with English Language and Literature.

Text Books for Normal and English Studies. Raub's Arithmetic, Monteith's Comprehensive Geography, Reed and Kellogg's Grammars and

Rhetoric, Anderson's United States History, Young's Civil Government, Hooker's Natural History, Wayland's Moral Science Abridged, Cutter's Physiology, Mayhew's Book-keeping, McGuffey's Readers, K dd's Elocution. Weekly elocutionary exercises and composition are required in all the courses of study, and also such study of the Bible as will enable the student to pass a creditable examination on Bible history and doctrines. Students are required to furn'sh themselves with reference Bibles, whenever practicable. Monthly written examinations of classes, in the course of study, is required, and at the end of each term students failing to get the minimum of sixty-five per cent., forfeit th ir standing in their classes.

The official summary shows the classification of the students; comparing the summary and the course of studies what they do is seen.

SUMMARY.

		MALES.	FEMALES.	TOTAL.
College Classes—Junior		0	1	1
	Sophomores	0	2	2
	Freshmen	5	2	7– 10
Preparatory	Third year	2	2	4
	Second year	13	3	16
	First year	12	3	15– 35
Academic	Th'rd year	1	1	2– 2
Normal	Third year, third grade	2	5	7
	Third year, second grade	17	6	23
	Third year, first grade	12	7	19
	Second year, third grade	9	5	14
	Second year, second grade	5	7	12
	Second year, first grade	16	22	38
	First year, third grade	3	3	6
	First year, second grade	20	21	41
	First year, first grade	39	36	75–235
Common English		16	29	45
Law		2	0	2
Medical	Seniors	8	0	8
	Juniors	23	0	23–31
Music		2	29	21-31
Theological		31	0	31-31
Total after omitting names counted twice.		207	153	360
Preparatory School at Mason		60	55	115
				475

There were eight graduates in 1884.

FACULTY.

J. Braden, D. D., President and Teacher of Mental and Moral Science ; Rev. W. Patterson, A. B , Teacher of Ancient Languages and Literature ; Charles T. Simpson A. B , Teacher of Ancient Languages and Mathematics; Rev. D. M. Birmingham, A. M. B. D , Dean of the Theological Department; G. W. Hubbard, M. D., Teacher of Natural Science ; E. M. Blakely, A. B., Assistant in Mathematics and Languages; D Moury and F H Curtiss, Principa's of the Normal Department, each part of year. Miss Lucy Hitchcock, Teacher in English and Formal Department; Miss S. A. Barnes, Preceptress and Teacher in Normal Depar ment; R. F. Boyd, M D , Teacher of Hygiene and Physiology : Miss M. E. Young, in charge of Model School; Miss M. E Braden and Mrs. L. C. Braden, Instrumental and Vocal Music; M ss R. Dodd, Matron; C. S. Randals, Superintendent of Industrial Department; Students in Normal School assistants in Model School.

SHAW UNIVERSITY, Raleigh, N. C , is one of the most vigorous and successful of the higher grade institutions for colored people in the South. It was founded in 1865 by the American Baptist Home Missionary Society. Its investments in real estate and improvements are worth $140,000. Shaw University has, besides the literary departments, schools of medicine and theology. Its industrial department is an important part of the institution and is, in many respects, worthy of imitation by other schools, whether for white or colored students.

The Catalogue for 1884 furnishes full information for the understanding of the character of the institution and its work. The organization of the corps of teachers in the literary departments is first presented.

In addition to the teaching force in the regular faculty thirty-two of the more advanced pupils, in 1884, rendered assistance, thus learning how to teach.

The studies pursued by the students of Shaw University are thus set forth in the annual announcement for 1884:

COURSE OF STUDY.

1. NORMAL COURSE—FIRST YEAR.

FIRST TERM.—Reading, Spelling, Penmanship, Arithmetic, Geography, Grammar.

SECOND TERM.—Reading, Spelling, Penmanship, Arithmetic, Geography, Grammar,

THIRD TERM.—Reading, Spelling, Penmanship, Arithmetic, Map Drawing, Grammar.

SECOND YEAR.

FIRST TERM.—Reading, Etymology, Penmanship, Arithmetic, Grammar.

SECOND TERM.—History, Reading, Etymology, Book-keeping, Arithmetic, Grammar

THIRD TERM.—History, Etymology, Book-Keeping, Arithmetic, Grammar, Physical Geog aphy.

THIRD YEAR.

FIRST TERM.—History, Etymology, Drawing, Algebra, English Analysis.

SECOND TERM.—Physiology, Hart's Composition, Geology, Algebra, English Analysis.

THIRD TERM.—Hart's Composition, Algebra, Botany, English Analysis, Lectures on the Principles and Methods of Teaching.

Rhetor cal exerci es every Wednesday afternoon; also instruction is given in the rudiments of vocal music.

2. SCIENTIFIC COURSE.

The first year's studies the same as in the Normal Course.

FOURTH YEAR.

First Term.—A'gebra, Rhetoric, Mental Philosophy.
Second Term.—Geo.etry, Moral Philosophy, Natural Philosophy.
Third Term.—Logic, Geometry, English Litera ure.

3. COLLEGE PREPARATORY COURSE.

FIRST YEAR.

First Term.—Latin . Harkness' First Latin Book. Mathematics: Arithmetic from per centage. English Grammar completed. Outlines of Ancient History and Geography.

Second Term.—Latin: Harkness' First Latin Book, completed. Mathematics: Arithmetic, Ancient History, English Composition.

Third Term.—Latin: Harkness' Latin Reader and Grammar. Mathematics: Arithmetic, completed. English Compo ition.

SECOND YEAR.

First Term.—Latin: Harkn ss' Latin Reader (Roman History.) Greek: Harkness' First Greek Book. Mathematics: Algebra.

Second Term.—Latin: Harkness' Latin Reader (Grecian History) Greek: Harkness' First Greek Book (continued.) Mathematics: Algebra. Hart's Rhetoric.

Third Term.—Latin: General Review of Latin Grammar. Greek: Harkness' First Greek Book, completed. Mathematics: Algebra. Hart's Rhetoric.

4. COLLEGE COURSE.

FRESHMAN YEAR.

First Term.—Latin: Harkness' Cæsar and Latin Prose Composition. Greek: Goodwin's Greek Grammar and Anabasis. Mathematics: Algebra, completed.

Second Term.—Latin: Harkness' Cæsar and Latin Prose Composition. Greek: Goodwin's Anabasis. Mathematics: Geometry.

Third Term.—Latin: Harkness' Cicero's Orations and Latin Prose Composition. Greek: Goodwin's Anabasis, completed. Mathematics: Geometry. Botany begun.

SOPHOMORE CLASS.

First Term.—Latin: Cicero's Orations Completed, Latin Prose Composition. Greek: Homer's Iliad. Mathematics: Trigonometry. Botany, completed.

Second Term.—Latin: Greenough's Virgil. Greek: Iliad, completed. Natural Philosophy and Zoology.

Third Term.—Latin: Virgil, completed. Greek: Greek Testament, Natural Philosophy and Zoology, comp eted.

JUNIOR CLASS.

First Term.—Latin: Cicero's De Senectute and De Amicitia; Greek: Greek Testament; Chemistry and Astronomy.

Second Term.—Latin: Livy; Logic; Chemistry and Astronomy, completed; Geology.

Third Term.—Latin: De Officiis; Geology; Political Economy.

SENIOR CLASS.

First Term.—Mineralogy; Mental Philosophy; Science of Government English Literature.

Second Term.—Moral Philosophy; History of Philosophy; English Literature.

Third Term.—Evidences of Christianity; Constitution of United States English Literature.

Weekly exercises in Declamations, Original Essays and Orations during entire course.

In the various departments of the school, all the different branches are taught, which a thorough course of study requires. There are six different departments, College, Scientific, Normal, Theological, Medical, and Industrial, in successful opera ion.

The courses of study in Normal Scientific, and College departments can be seen by referring to another page.

THEOLOGICAL DEPARTMENT.—The Theological Department comprises the regular course of two years for students who have graduated from the Academical Department, and the English course for those who have not completed their literary studies. Dr. Hovey's Outlines of Theology will be used as a text-book in the regular course. Interpretation of Scripture will receive special attention as affording the only true basis for theological study. There will be classes in both Greek and Hebrew, that students may be able to read the Scriptures in the original.   In Homiletics students will receive instruction in the work of sermon-making. Instruction will be given by the Faculty in Evidences of Christianity, Biblical Instruction, History of Doctrine, Church History, Church Polity and Pastoral Duties. The text-books in the English course will be Pendleton's Christian Doctrines. The other studies will be the same as in the regular course.

MEDICAL DEPARTMENT.—Two large buildings known as the Medical Dormitory and Leonard Medical Building have been erected; the latter adorns the beautiful site so generously donated by the State of North Carolina. The buildings are commodious and will afford first-class accommodations for a full course in medicine. The Department of Medical instruction has been provided for, and the Trustees and Faculty will put forth every effort possible to make this department of study of great value to the colored people. The Annual Course of Lectures will commence November first and continue five months.

The official summary gives the classification of the pupils. It is as follows :

GRADUATES OF THE UNIVERSITY.

THEOLOGICAL DEPARTMENT.
May, 1884.

L. T. CHRISTMAS, ... Warrenton, N. C.
A. J. EDWARDS, ... R'ch Square, N. C.

SCIENTIFIC COURSE.
J. W. POPE, ... Plymouth, N. C.

ESTEY SEMINARY.
MISS HATTIE WILSON, ... Durham, N. C.

SUMMARY.
Normal Course.

Males, ...	171
Females, ...	158
	—— 330

Scientific Course.

Males, ...	11
Females, ...	7
	— 48

Classical Course.

Males, ...	45
Females, ...	3
	— 48

Medical Course.

Males, ...	21

Model School.

Males, ...	11
Females, ...	14
	— 25

School of Carpentry and Furniture-Making, ...	120
School of Dress-Making and Domestic Arts, ...	121

Music Only.

Females, ...   2

Total males, ...   224
Total females, ...   185
                                                  — 429
Total studying for the Ministry, ...   55

In 1884 there were two graduates from the theological department, one from the scientific, and one from Estey Seminary—the name of a "department" in the literary course.

The TUSKEGEE STATE NORMAL SCHOOL, Tuskegee, Ala., may well represent the work of institutions of this class. This school was established by act of the Legislature of Alabama in 1880, and receives from the State $3 000 per annum. The institution owns a farm of 580 acres and improvements, worth about $25,000. Its efficient and respected Principal, Rev. B. T. Washington, himself a colored man and a graduate of Hampton Institute, commands approval by his good sense, his fidelity, his capacity and his success. The Catalogue for 1884 shows officers and teachers, 10; students, 169. The teachers and their positions are as follows:

OFFICERS AND TEACHERS.

B. T. WASHINGTON, Principal; Mental and Moral Science, Rhetoric, Grammar and Composition. MISS OLIVIA A. DAVIDSON, Assistant Principal; Mathematics, Astronomy and Botany. WARREN LOGAN, Natural Sciences, Literature and Bookkeeping. M. J. MADDOX, Elocution and History. WM. JENKINS, Mathematics and Brass Band Instructor. MISS ROSA MASON, Matron; Spelling, Geography and Penmanship. MISS ADELLA HUNT, Didactics, Principal of Training School and Librarian. MISS ADDIE J. WALLACE, Assistant in Training School and in charge of Girls' Industrial Department. HENRY C. FERGUSON, Farm Manager and General Superintendent of Industries. MRS. FANNY N. WASHINGTON, Housekeeper.

The studies pursued are thus described:

COURSE OF STUDY.

The regular course of instruction extends through a period of four years.

JUNIOR YEAR.

Language.—Elocution: Physical and vocal drill. Orthography: Spelling and dictation exercises (both written) and punctuation. Composition:

3

Original composition, oral and written, including sentence-making, business and friendly letters and composition on general topics, abstracts. Grammar: Analysis of sentences, parsing.

Mathematics.—Mental and Written Arithmetic: Mental: Analysis and numeral combinations; Written: Robinson's Practical Arithmetic from factoring to applications of denominate numbers.

Geometry.—Study of lines and angles and common forms of surfaces and solids.

Geography.—Study of natural and political divisions of land and water, commercial geography, special study of the geography and history of Alabama, and map drawing.

History.—History and outline of the form of government of the United States. Lives and characters of prominent persons connected with each period.

Writing.—Spencerian copy books.

Calisthenics.

Vocal Music.

B. MIDDLE YEAR.

Language.—Elocution: Physical and vocal drill, phonetics, and examples and definitions of different qualities of voice. Orthography: Written, spelling and dictation exercises and punctuation. Composition: Oral and written, including writing and telling simple stories, writing business and friendly letters, composition on general topics, and abstracts. Grammar: Analysis and parsing, simple figures of speech.

Mathematics.—Mental and Written Arithmetic and Algebra.

Geometry.—Inventional: Text, Spencer's Science Primer.

Geography.—Mathematical and Physical: First half the year.

Astronomy.—Simple lessons in, during the last half of the year. Text, Lockyer's Science Primer.

History.—Universal: Outline of.

Physiology and Hygiene.

Vocal Music.

Writing.—Spencerian copy books.

Calisthenics.

A. MIDDLE YEAR.

Language.—Elocution. Orthography. Composition: Oral and written. Rhetoric.

Literature.—Study of lives and principal works of American authors.

Mathematics.—Written Arithmetic and Algebra, completed.

Geometry.

Geometrical Drawing.

Free-Hand Drawing.

Natural Philosophy.

History.—Review of American history in connection with contemporary English.

Zoology and Botany.—Elementary lessons in.

Vocal Music.

Calisthenics.

Literature.—Study of lives and works of English authors.

Mathematics.—Review of Arithmetic; bookkeeping.

Geometry.

Free Hand Drawing.

Methods of Teaching.

Civil Government.—Special study of the Constitution of the United States, and of the school laws of Alabama.

Chemistry.

Mental and Moral Philosophy.

Calisthenics.

Vocal Music.

In the model school connected with the Normal, two regular teachers are employed, under whom the students receive practical training as teachers.

Lectures on current topics are given throughout the course.

A few students, with no money, work all day and attend night school. In this way they earn money with which to pay their expenses in the day school the succeeding term.

There are hundreds of institutions, North and South, to which students can go and receive mental training, but those where young men and women can learn a *trade* in addition to other training are few. At present the industries of the institution are farming, brick-making, carpentering, printing, blacksmithing; and housekeeping and sewing for girls.

To these the institution expects to add tin-smithing, shoe-making, painting, broom-making, etc.

For the impetus given to the industrial department of the school, it is indebted chiefly to the "John F. Slater Fund."

This department is carried on with almost no loss to the student in his classses.

It is instructive and encouraging to add what the principal says of

WORK.

"Work is required of all for the purpose of discipline and instruction and of teaching the dignity of labor."

The official summary will show the classification of the students in Tuskegee State Normal School.

SUMMARY.

A. *Middle Class.*—Girls 5, Boys 5; B. *Middle Class.*—Girls 10, Boys 14; *Junior Class.*—Girls 18, Boys 40; *Preparatory Class.*—Girls 36, Boys 41; Total 169.

Similar illustrations might be given from the records and announcements of all the higher grade schools for colored people in the Southern States, but those presented here are fairly representative and illustrative of them all. The schools aided by the John F. Slater Fund for the school year 1883-'84 are the following:

INSTITUTIONS.	LOCATIONS.	AMOUNTS GIVEN.
Clark University	Atlanta, Ga	$2.000
Tuskegee State Normal School	Tuskegee, Ala	1,100
LeMoyne Institute	Memphis, Tenn	500
Claflin University	Orangeburg, S. C	2,000
Talladega College	Talladega, Ala	2 000
Shaw University	Raleigh, N. C	2,000
Leonard Medical School	Raleigh, N. C	500
Touga'oo University	Tougaloo, Ala	2 000
Hampton Normal Institute	Hampton Va	2,000
Lewis Normal School	Macon, Ga	200
Atlanta University	Atlanta Ga	2 000
Brainerd Institute	Chester, S. C	750
Spelman Female Seminary	Atlanta Ga	2 000
Rush University	Holly Springs, Miss	1,600
Central Tennessee College	Nashville, Tenn	500
Meharry Medical College	Nashville, Tenn.	500
Southern University	New Orleans, La	250
LeLand University	New Orleans, La	341.61
Tillotson Institute	Austin, Tex	600.—
Scotia Seminary	Concord, N C	240.—
Fisk University	Nashville, Tenn	1,975
Roger Williams University	Nashville, Tenn	1,350
Lincoln Normal University	Marion Ala	450

In these schools there were employed, during the school years 1883-'84, 303 teachers; there were enrolled 7,273 students. The percentage of the whole number engaged in classical studies and the higher mathematics and other college studies and studies preparatory to admission to the college classes was very small—*less than five per cent. of the whole number.* And fully one-half of these were not advanced beyond the requisites for admission into the Freshman classes in the better grade colleges for white students.

Of under education and of bad education we see abundant proof in the schools for both races; over education is a very remote danger. More colored men and women, prepared for educational leadership by the training and culture of the higher studies, will be needed than can for a long

time be supplied by all the schools that give opportunity
to the very few who can pursue the higher studies.

Rev. Dr. Rust, in his report in 1881, made the following
statement :

"Seventy-five thousand pupils, according to our best estimate, have been taught in our schools of various grades
since we entered upon this work for the freedmen. It is
estimated that three-fourths of a million (750,000) of children in the South have been taught by the teachers of our
schools and by our pupils who have engaged in teaching."
That is the officers of the Freedmen's Aid Society and of
the institutions under its patronage estimated, in 1881,
that 675,000 colored children had been taught by teachers
instructed in these schools. There is no reason to question
their estimate, and similar estimates would be justified as
to the work of the schools under the other great societies
and of the schools established by State authority.

The possibility of such results appears when it is considered that the average cost to students in these schools is
$1.00 per month for tuition and $8.50 per month for board.

Take the following named States : Alabama, Florida,
Georgia, Kentucky, Louisiana, Mississippi, North Carolina,
South Carolina, Tennessee, Texas and Virginia, and the
Tenth Census, volume 1, page 917, shows that the average
monthly pay of teachers in the public schools was $26.90,
and the average amount paid each teacher (in 1880) was
$111.54. The colored teachers do as well as the white, and
these colored students of the advanced classes do what
thousands of white boys and girls do—make enough in the
public schools, during vacation, to continue at school, with
such other small aid as they can procure.

The President of Shaw University, the Rev. Dr. H. M.
Tupper, says that more than 1,000 of his former students
are so engaged. Over 400 who have gone out from Rust
University are in this work. Most of the more advanced
pupils teach while going to school—using the long vaca-
tions to secure funds to continue their own studies. In
1883, 124 of the students then at Fisk University had been
teaching in the public schools, and more than that num-

ber were teaching in the vacation that followed. In the
Atlanta University, the same year, there were 200 of these
teacher students. In Central Tennessee College, seven-
eighths of the more advanced students were teaching while
studying. The President of Howard University, the Rev.
Dr. W. M. Patton, wrote your Agent, in 1883, that "90 per
cent." of his graduates and advanced pupils were teachers·
Your Agent is informed by the President of Central Tennessee College, the Rev. Dr. John Braden, that more than
1200 men and women, taught in that institution, are teaching the children of their people.

WHAT THEY ARE DOING.

Men and women who have attended these schools and
schools like them are all over the South, teaching colored
children. Beyond comparison they are the best colored
teachers engaged in this work. It is impossible to give an
accurate statement of the number now teaching in the
colored schools, and doing more to reduce colored illiteracy
than all other teachers. But some statements, justified by
official and reliable information, will indicate the extent of
the work now being done by colored teachers trained in
these higher grade schools; these statements vindicate the
wisdom of Mr. Slater in indicating his desire that the funds
accruing from his gift of a million of dollars, should be so
used as to aid in training teachers.

THE WEAKNESS OF THE COLORED SCHOOLS IN THE SOUTH

Is in the material upon which they work. This weakness
is in the antecedents and present status of the race. He is
no friend to the colored race who would try to sentimental-
ize out of view the sad facts of their case. No amount of
money, no perfection of method, no expenditure of energy
can at once, or within a generation, or within two gener-
ations, eradicate the difficulties that inhere in the heredities
and social conditions that make the case of the negroes in the
Southern States what it is. The work must be done in
spite of these difficulties. And the right principle of ac-
tion in such a case is, where a great and necessary work
is to be done, and it is not only difficult but of such nature

that it must take a very long time to accomplish it, and it is so connected with the very roots of social order and progress that failure means disaster, then, the sooner this work is begun and the more earnestly it is pressed the better for all concerned.

None can fully understand what is meant by the "weakness" of the "material" upon which the teachers in these colored schools are engaged, who are ignorant of the negro's condition as to education when in slavery, who do not know how poor they are to day, who do not know, by close and long observation, the limitations that compass them about on every side.

A GREAT TASK NOBLY UNDERTAKEN.

There was never before such an educational duty as that which, by the results of the war between the States, was thrown upon the conscience of patriotic, humane and Christian people in the United States. In a few months four millions of people who had been slaves were made citizens. There was never an educational task so grave and so urgent. Never was a great duty so nobly attempted. It would take a volume to give a faithful outline of the history.

The work of giving Christian education to the negro race in the South was commenced September 17, 1861, under the auspices of the American Missionary Association, at Hampton, Virginia. "Its first teacher," says the Rev. Dr. M. E. Strieby, Corresponding Secretary of the Association, "was Mrs. Mary S. Peake, a very intelligent Christian woman, who represented the white and the colored races, and who had, in some way, obtained an education before the war." Before the end of the war nearly all the churches of the Northern States were in the field; they have been there ever since; they will be needed there a long time.

To show how rapidly the work grew under the hands of its first projectors, and to show what sort of people entered upon it, a paragraph may be quoted from an address delivered by Dr. Strieby, at Ocean Grove, New Jersey, August,

1883, at a meeting of the National Educational Assmbly. Dr. Strieby said:

At the end of the war the Association had enlisted the sympa'hies of the peop'e on both sides of the ocean, and had greatly enlarged its work ; so that its receipts, which were only $65,000 for the year before the war, reached $250,000 for the year after the war, and its teachers sent to the freedmen in 1866 numbered 320. These teachers deserve special mention. Most of them were ladies, and were from the best Christian families of the north; many of them had won distinction in the best schools there, and in the spirit of the highest Christian self sacrifice, they left honored social positions, the comforts and embellishments of refined homes, and gave themselves, sometimes without compensation and always with very meagre salaries, to the privation, ostracism and danger of their new posi.ion.

This language will tell the history of most of the other societies that have engaged in this work. During the last twenty years the number of teachers, the majority being ladies all along, runs up into thousands and the sums expended into millions. Counting the appropriations made by the Government through the Freedmen's Bureau, those made by the great societies, as the American Missionary Association, the Freedmen's Aid Society, the Presbyterian Board of Missions for Freedmen, the American Baptist Home Mission Society, the appropriations made by the Protestant Episcopal Church, the Unitarians and the Friends, and adding to these appropriations the gifts of individuals, not reported in the annual publications of the benevolent societies, there is reason to believe that from the year 1861, when this work was commenced, to date, the sum of not less than $40,000,000 has been invested in the work of educating and christianizing the enfranchised negroes of the Southern States.

To indicate the extent of the effort that is now being made, a few statements may be made of the amounts expended by some of the leading societies engaged in the work. Data are lacking for a statement that will include them all.

For the school year 1883-84 the American Baptist Home Mission Society expended over $150,000 upon schools for the freedmen. The appropriations for the current year for

this work by the American Missionary Association amount
to $202,211.80. The expenditures of the Freedmen's Aid
Society for the year ending July 1, 1884, amounted to $147,-
652.79, of which about $125,000 was expended for the ben-
efit of freedmen's schools. The Presbyterian Board of Missions for freedmen expended on institutions for teaching
the colored people for the school year 1883-84 $33,377.79.
Add to these amounts the expenditures of the other societies, the amounts appropriated from the Peabody Fund and
the John F. Slater Fund, and special gifts of individuals to
the different schools, and the aggregate will not be far from
$1,000.000 for the current year.

The Southern States expended in 1882, as shown in the
Report of the Commissioner, the sum of $14,820,972 on its
public schools—the races sharing alike under school laws
that make no distinction between them. These are
large sums, but the school population is larger; the need
of money is great; the churches and benevolent societies,
aided by the occasional large gifts of generous individuals,
are not able to do the work that must be done; the South-
'ern States are not able, by unaided effort, to carry this
burden. Every day strengthens the argument for national
aid.

While the scope and design of this paper does not con-
template an argument on the subject of national aid to
education, a few general statements may be made.

Many persons think that the Southern States are far
behind their duty in their expenditures on public schools.
An increasing number of Southern men think they ought
to do more than they are doing, but when the facts are considered, they are doing more than they have generally received credit for doing.

The total expenditure for public schools in the United
States was, in round numbers, in 1880, $83,000,000; in 1880
the Southern States expended on public schools, in round
numbers, $13,000,000, or something over $1 00 in every
$7.00. These summaries do not by any means fairly rep-
resent the actual work done in Southern public schools, or
the amounts expended upon them. It is the custom to sup-

plement the school fund by subscriptions of patrons, in order to secure more competent teachers and to extend the term. As illustrative: the Hon. H. C. Armstrong, late Superintendent of Public Schools in Alabama, in 1882, reported to the Commissioner at Washington that in "twenty counties of Alabama the public school fund was supplemented by patrons to the extent of $66,990, and in forty-six other counties by an amount equal probably to $175,000." The amount of expenditures by the State for 1881 was $403,602; add the amounts reported by Mr. Armstrong and we have nearly $650,000.

In 1880 the total valuation of taxable property in the United States was $16,902,995,543; the thirteen States grouped as "Southern States" in the census tables, show a total valuation of taxable property of $2,370,923,269—or a little more than $1.00 in every $7.00.

A few illustrative comparisons will throw some light on the subject. Thus: the Tenth Census shows the valuation of taxable property of the State of New York to be $2,651,-940,006. The total expenditures of New York for 1880 on public schools was $9.936,662. The total taxable property of the Southern Division of States was $261,020,737 less than that of New York; yet these States expended on their public schools in 1880 $12 475,044; in 1881 $13,359,784; in 1882, $14,820,972.

An illustration is given in "Circular No. 4, 1884," from the Bureau of Education) page 94: "Take North Carolina and Massachusetts as the units of measure. In 1880 the taxable property of Massachusetts was $1,600,000,000, and the school tax was $4,000,000; that is, Massachusetts pays $1.00 a year out of every $400 of taxable property. In 1880 the taxable property of North Carolina was $160,000,000, and the school tax was $400,000, that is, $1 00 out of every $400 of taxable property, which is exactly what Massachusetts pays."

Mere figures cannot state the truth in such comparisons; it is harder to give a little out of a little than much out of much. The best test of liberality and public spirit is in what is left rather than in what is given. From 1870 to 1880, to say nothing of the decade between 1860 and 1870, there was a decrease in the value of property in every Southern State except Georgia, North Carolina and Texas. If we consider the waste and shrinkage of values from 1860 to 1880, the amounts are prodigious. In an address before the Social Science Association, at Saratoga, September, 1877, Dexter A. Hawkins, Esq., of New York city, stated the case thus:

"The assessed valuation for the taxation of property, real and personal, in North Carolina, South Carolina, Florida, Georgia, Alabama, Mississippi, Louisiana and Texas, in 1860 was $3,244,239,406; in 1870, $1,883,863,180, a shrinkage in ten years of 43¼ per cent."

Mayor Courtnay, of the city of Charleston, S. C., has given the subject of public education much intelligent attention. In making a plea for national aid, he puts the case thus:

The facts are these: In the first place, the assessed values in the city of Charleston were $45,000,000 in 1860; in 1880, $21,000,000—a reduction of more than one-half in the taxable values, in the face of an obligation to educate double the number of children.

This heavy load has been assumed up to the highest pitch of taxation, however, as the facts show. The taxation in the city of Charleston, in 1880, for public schools, was three and one-half mills, made up under a levy of two mills under the State law, one and one-quarter mills under the special city tax, and one-quarter mill special levy to rebuild Friend Street school—in all amounting to about $61,000 a year on public schools. And this is exclu ive of an annual appropriation to the high school of Charleston and to Charleston College.

How much above a maximum this is, and what a burden this is, is evident upon comparison. For instance, compare this taxation with the city of Boston, whose schools are models, and whose people have the world-wide reput t'on of giving liberally for educational institutions, and we find that the city of Boston gives a total of two and a half mills in 1880 for a complete public school establishment, of seven high schoo's, two Latin schools, one normal school, forty-nine grammar schools, and four hundred and eight primary schools. The city of Charleston gives in proportion nearly half as much again as Boston for her primary schools alone, and giv s, in addition, annual appropriati ms to the high school and Charleston College.

We must remember, also, that this is done under a heavy debt of the city, the interest of which requires ten mills of annual taxation. Again, consider that, besides the State tax, the total tax of Charleston city is 2½ per cent., while that of Boston is only 1⅝ per cent."

Table IX, in Appendix, will give very full information on some of the points brought forward in the foregcing statements. These figures show in a very clear light both the poverty and the burdens of the Southern division of States. Comparing tables IX and I, we see how poverty and sparseness of population, and a vast area of territory increase the difficulties of the situation. In this connection it may be stated, as throwing some further light on the subject, that there is very little non-taxable wealth in the Southern States. Thus of 73,114 persons holding United States bonds in 1880 there are, in the States of Virginia, Tennessee, Louisiana, Mississippi, North Carolina, South Carolina, Alabama, Arkansas, Florida, Georgia, only 1851. In Massachusetts there are 16,855 bondholders; in Georgia 58. The amount of the bonds held in Massachusetts is $45,138,750, in Georgia $181,400. In New York there are 14,803 bondholders, in Arkansas 78; amount in New York $210,264,250, in Arkansas $312,400.

A grave difficulty that increases the cost of reaching a given number of scholars, and makes it impossible to reach thousands of them without largely increased resources, is in the vast extent of the Southern territory and its sparse population. (Table 1 in Appendix will show in figures the nature and extent of this difficulty.)

But there is promise of improvement even here. The settlement of the country and the breaking up of the large plantations means better times. The census shows a great increase of proprietors. For illustration, five States are taken; the number of proprietors about doubled from 1870 to 1880. To show the relation of this tendency to the state of things following emancipation, the figures are given for 1860 and 1850 :

States.	1880.	1870.	1860.	1850.
Alabama	135,861	67,382	55,128	41,964
Arkansas	94,433	49,424	39,004	17,758
Georgia	138,626	69,956	62,003	51,759
Florida	23,438	10,241	6,508	4,304
South Carolina	93,864	51,389	33,171	29,967

Another doubling will accomplish many revolutions, industrial, social, educational and political, bringing untold blessings to the people. For one thing, an efficient common school system will not only be a felt necessity, it will be a possibility.

Another fact to be considered, in reaching just conclusions on this subject, is that what is paid by the South to the public schools, with the exception of a few States, must all of it come directly out of the pockets of the people. According to the American Almanac for 1879 the Northern States have received more than 70,000,000 acres of public lands, which, at the government price amounts to $88,000,000; the South has received only six and a half millions of acres, amounting in round numbers to $8,000,000, a difference of $80,000,000 in favor of the States that did not grow poor by the results of the war, and that did not have thrown upon them the burden of educating the children of over six millions of people, virtually non-tax-payers. Representative illustrations of the last allusion may be offered. Rev. Dr. J. L. M. Curry, in an address at Louisville, Ky., September, 1883, very tersely stated the case when he said:

The negroes, who, in some of the States are a majority of the population, are poor, and pay a very small part of the taxes. The aggregate value of the whole property of colored tax-payers in Georgia was $6,590,876, while the total taxable property was $287,269,403. The Comptroller of South Carolina is confident that the white people in the State pay nine-tenths of the taxes. In Wilmington, North Carolina, the negroes outnumber the whites in about the ratio of eleven to eight. Of about every $12 of the school fund, the whites pay $11 and the negroes $1, and yet of these $12 the negroes get $8.50 and the whites $3.50. In Danville, Va., the city taxes in 1882, exclusive of license tax for corporate uses, were about $40,000, of which $1,206.63 were paid by negroes. In Kentucky the apportionment of school fund, at the rate of $1.40 per capita, to colored children, is $129,438. The taxes, together with all the fines and forfeitures collected from the negroes, are devoted to the education of colored children, and yet there is a deficit in the colored school fund of $92,345.36.

These things are not said to their disparagement. Their poverty is not of their creating. Suffrage in their hands is exceptionally dangerous, because, elated by the suddenness and manner of their liberation, unacquainted with the responsibilities of freedom, crazed by vague and false notions of liberty, they may be easily deluded by bad men.

A PROBLEM WITHOUT ANY MYSTERY.

There are many grounds for encouragement. The per centage of illiteracy actually decreased among the colored people between 1870 and 1880. In no possible sense has the great effort to educate them been a failure; it has, judged by any rational test, been a marvelous success.

It has been a success if we consider how many of them have learned to read and to write; if we consider how much better they behave as free people than was expected in 1865: if we consider how steadily the hundreds of thousands of them make progress in true civilization; if we consider that they are beginning to appear on the tax books as owners of houses and little farms; if we consider what crops they make every year, in spite of a badly organized farming system; if we consider the marked advance in sensible preaching evinced by the colored preachers, and the earnest effort of the colored churches to raise the standard of practical morals.

More and more Southern public opinion approves the education of the colored people; more and more right methods of teaching them are coming into use. The facts show that education tends to do for the negroes what it tends to do for all people, to make them better people.

The experiment has not gone far enough to have collected ample statistics to demonstrate the effect of education upon negro character. In so wide a field a theorist can find some facts to sustain any view. *The good that comes through education depends upon the education.* It was the desire of the noble founder of the fund this board is called on to administer, that his great gift should be used to foster "Christian education" among the "lately emancipated people and their descendants" in the Southern States.

An education un-Christian would be fatal to these people; an education simply not Christian would fail to save them from the perils of their position. They must be educated in sound morals, and this will come through Christian education.

The Board may rest assured that the institutions to

which money from the John F. Slater Fund has been appropriated are under Christian influence.

The influences that characterize a school, whether it be a very humble grammar school or a great university, are determined, not by the theory upon which the school was founded, but by the personal character of the teachers who manage it. Large opportunity for forming an opinion gives me great confidence in saying that, as a rule, the men and women who are engaged in the higher grade schools for colored people are sensible, practical and religious in the best sense. Mistakes many of them may have made, but the gracious results that have been accomplished show how wisely, as well as earnestly, most of them have done their work. More and more do they realize the truth so tersely stated by General S. C. Armstrong in an address reported in the Richmond *Whig*, February 28, 1883. General Armstrong said:

"It is not a question of brain with the black man. It is easy for them to acquire knowledge, but to attain a character is a very different thing. To educate them wisely, properly, requires attention to the whole routine of daily life. It is a matter of good habits rather than of mere book knowledge. The Hampton School is founded on this idea. It is to create men and women rather than polished scholars; men who shall be the pioneers of their civilization."

More and more investigation makes it clear that Mr. Slater, in his letter to the gentlemen composing this Board, clearly apprehended the question of the education of the colored race in the Southern States. A quotation from that letter is appropriate and instructive here:

"But it is not only for their own sake, but also for the sake of our common country, in which they have been invested with equal political rights, that I am desirous to aid in providing them with the means of such education as shall tend to make them good men and good citizens—education in which the instruction of the n. .id 'ɔ the common branches of secular learning shall be associated with training in just notions of duty toward God and man in the light of the Holy Scriptures. The means to be used in the prosecution of the general object above described, I leave to the discretion of the corporation, only indicating as lines of operation adapted to the present condition of things. the training of teachers from among the people requiring to be taught, if in the opinion of the corporation, by such limited selection the purposes of the trust can be best accomplished; and the encouragement of such institutions as are most effectually useful in promoting this training of teachers."

In seeking to carry out Mr. Slater's wise and generous designs this Board, at it smeeting in New York city, April 26, 1883, unanimously adopted a resolution which indicates the best possible method of accomplishing the donor's purpose. The resolution reads:

"Resolved, That, for the present, this Board confine its aid to such schools as are best fitted to prepare young colored men and women to become useful to their race; and that institutions which give instruction in trades and other manual occupations, that will enable colored youths to make a living, and to become useful citizens, be carefully sought out and preferred in appropriations from this fund; and that, so far as practicable, the scholars receiving aid from this foundation shall be trained to some manual occupation simultaneously with their mental and moral instruction."

The appropriations that have been made by your Agent have been made in accordance with the spirit of this resolution. More worthy institutions are ready and eager to work in harmony with this plan than can be aided unless the funds available were twice or thrice what they are. The results of the policy pursued are so far good; they will be better with more effort and experience.

Mr. Slater, in his first letter to the members of this Board, showed that he had made himself familiar with the history and character of the good work he desired to aid. He was right when he said:

' I am well aware that the work herein proposed is nothing new or untried."

There is, perhaps, no missionary work going on in the

Christian world that is so well understood and there is certainly none that offers speedier or ampler success to those who are engaged in it. The people we serve are in our midst; they know our language; they are bound to us by a thousand sympathies and relations; they know our institutions beyond comparison better than any people needing missionary work ever knew the institutions of those who undertook their Christianization. These people have had much training in systematic labor; many of them already have trades which support them and every test shows them capable of improvement.

We must not forget the preparatory work that was done among these people before schools were opened for their instruction in books. If the Southern church has done little since the war, it did much before the war. All these people, through the missionary agencies of the Southern church, knew something of Christianity; thousands upon thousands of them were Christians. The astonishing progress that has been made among the colored people of the South, since their freedom, was made possible by what had been done for them before their freedom.

Few things could be more unfortunate for the work this Board has in hand than to enter upon it with the feeling that a very uncertain experiment is to be made. There is no mystery whatever in the education of the negro race; it is a question of money more than anything else. The negro is to be taught the things he needs to know to make him all he is capable of becoming. Money will provide the means and instrumentalities for doing the work; there are capable men and women enough who will work in this field for moderate support. The negro youth needs what the white youth needs—knowledge, industry, morals. The schools at work in the Southern States are teaching him books, they are teaching him sound morals, they are begining to teach him tool-craft. What he learns of one will help him to learn the others, and learning each he will begin to make greater progress in all good things. Nothing in the history of the educational movement for the uplifting of

4

the negroes is more encouraging than the growing interest
in the work that is being manifested by the superior white
people of the South. This growing sentiment is recognized
by some who have the management of the higher grade
schools for colored people in hand; Southern names begin
to appear in the lists of trustees and managers. It would
be very wise, at this time, to increase their number.

The proof of this growing interest is abundant and con-
clusive. If the work is ever to be done as the needs of
both races require that it be done, then the time must come
when Southern white people cordially co-operate in the
work. It would be as easy to develop a colony into a great
State by immigration alone, in a country without births,
as to permanently establish and successfully conduct a
great educational work by supplies from abroad. Perhaps
it may turn out that one. of the best results the John F.
Slater Fund can accomplish through its management will
be the fostering of interest in the work of educating the
negro among those white people whose interest in his right
education is greater than that of any other white people—
whose interest in making of the negro a good citizen is only
less than the interest of the negro himself in his own ele-
vation.

APPENDIX.

TABLE 1.—*The Area and Population, the Population to square mile and the White and Colored Population by States and Territories, and Sex, 1880.*

States and Territories.	Area in square miles.	Population	Population to square mile.	RACE.			
				White.		Colored.	
				Male.	Female.	Male.	Female.
Alabama	51,740	1 262 5 5	24.50	327 517	334,668	295,10	305,102
Arkansas	53,04	8 2,22	15.13	30,766	282,825	107,331	103,335
California	155,980	864,694	5. 4	43 , 56	33 125	3,467	2,551
Colorado	103,64	194, 27	1.87	127,741	64,08	1,433	1,002
Connecticut	4,845	62.,700	128.5	299,940	311,789	5,5 0	5,997
Delaware	1,900	146,0 8	74.8	60,7.7	59.488	13,327	13,115
Florida	54,24	264 498	4.97	73,2 4	6,341	6 ,068	63,622
Georgia	58. 0	1, 4 1 0	26, 5	403,741	413, 6	359 157	365,976
Illinois	56,00 0	3,07 7.87	4 9	1,561,7.6	1,469 4 5	24,5 7	21,861
Indiana	35 9 0	1,978.3 1	55.09	98,9 3	945,84	20,267	18,961
Iowa	55,475	1,02,615	29. 9	842,6 4	771 906	5 191	4,325
Kansas	8,70	9 6 696	12 19	511,184	438,71	22,152	20,935
Kentucky	4 0 0	1,6 86.0	41,22	698,7 7	675,422	1 3,798	137,653
Louisiana	45,420	939 946	2 6	2.8.97	22,98	238,879	244,776
Maine	29 89	6 48 986	21.71	3.2 973	323 879	765	686
Maryland	9,860	934,943	84 82	359.6 0	86 ,025	102,505	107,725
Massachusetts	8 040	1,78 ,80	221.78	848,977	9 4.80	9 0 9	9,648
Michigan	5 ,43	1,649,987	18.6	850,795	763. 65	7,836	7,264
Minnesota	79,205	780.773	9,86	417,075	359,800	90	659
Mississippi	46 340	1 1 ,597	24.42	243.226	236, 72	322,939	327,382
Missouri	68,735	2,1 ,380	31.55	1,54,879	967,917	72,153	73,197
Nebraska	76,8	452,40	5 94	247 8	2 1 949	1,296	1,089
Nevada	109,740	62,26	0.57	35,059	18,497	308	180
New Hampshire	9,05	346,991	8.53	170.13	176,49	341	344
New Jersey	7,455	1,131,11	151.73	540,87	551 47	18,846	20,007
New York	47 620	5, 8 871	106,74	2 473,121	2,542,401	30,82	34,252
North Carolina	48,580	1,399,7 0	28,80	4 4,011	4 2,98	262,363	268,914
Ohio	40,760	3,1 8. 6	78 46	1,572,789	1,545,131	40,962	35,938
Oregon	94,560	74.76	1 8	92 93	70,140	270	217
Pennsylvania	44 98	4,282,	95.2	2 095,213	2,104 80	41,193	44,342
Rhode Island	1 08	276. 31	54.8	13 , 4	139,9 5	2,952	3,536
South Carolina	30,170	9 5 57	3 .0	192 544	198, 61	297,787	304,545
Tennessee	4 ,7	1 54 3 9	36,94	57 .6 3	56 ,22	197,467	205,684
Texas	262 29	1,591.74	6.07	6 0,69	55 798	196,746	196,648
Vermont	9 43	32,.86	36 8	166,8 2	164 906	566	401
Virginia	40.12	1,51 ,765	37.7	4 6,6	4 4,227	308,93	322,681
West Virginia	24 645	618 457	25 09	30 ,99.	291, 1	13 482	12,404
Wisconsin	54 450	1 315,49	24.16	676,949	632,669	1,521	1,181
Total	2 040 78	49 371 40	24, 9	21,73 21	2 976 264	3,225,87	3,293,185
Arizona	112 9 6	40 440	0,36	24,5	19 6 4	104	51
Dakota	147 50	13 ,17	0.92	81 76	51,971	225	176
District of Columbia	60	177 624	2960. 10	57.320	60,686	26,288	33,358
Idaho	84 29	3 6 4	0. 9	18,410	10,573	33	14
Montana	145 310	39,59	0 27	2 22	9,-63	191	155
New Mexico	122 4	9,565	0.9	58,65	50 166	638	377
Utah	82,190	143 963	1.7	73.177	68,946	124	108
Washington	66,8 0	5 1 5	1.1	4 . 13	26,686	209	116
Wyoming	97,87	0.75	0. 1	13,026	6 411	16	138
Total	856,33	7 4 3	0.9	32,685	295,806	27,9 8	34,493
Grand total	2 900,17	50 ,7 3	7.	1 0 9 0	21 272.07	3, 53, 15	3,3 7,678

TABLE II—*The number, nativity, and race of the legal school population of each State and Territory in 1880.*

States and Territories.	Native White.	Foreign White.	Total White.	Colored. a	Total.
Alabama	213,493	659	214,152	208,587	422,739
Arkansas	210,891	1,127	212,018	76,834	288,862
California	184,309	9,100	193,409	7,874	201,283
Colorado	39,710	3,594	43,304	794	44,098
Connecticut	134,699	8,754	143,453	2,556	146,009
Delaware	38,842	779	39,621	9,268	48,889
Florida	57,585	1,416	59,001	56,495	115,496
Georgia	229,592	380	229,872	231,144	461,016
Illinois	983,977	74,583	1,058,559	15,276	1,073,835
Indiana	682,616	12,107	694,723	13,459	708,182
Iowa	579,574	37,417	616,991	3,609	620,600
Kansas	348,867	20,27-	359,145	17,406	376,551
Kentucky	474,409	2,806	477,216	71,807	548,522
Louisiana	127,722	1,502	129,224	142,190	271,414
Maine	205,889	13,636	219,525	669	220,194
Maryland	239,362	6,647	245,009	74,192	319,201
Massachusetts	302,879	26,832	3.9,711	3,309	333,020
Michigan	460,582	65,652	526,234	7,529	533,763
Minnesota	237,867	49,790	287,657	1,371	289,028
Mississippi	185,484	617	186,101	272,754	458,855
Missouri	673,181	15,223	688,404	50,308	738,712
Nebraska	140,077	20,960	161,037	861	161,898
Nevada	8,567	723	9,290	839	10,129
New Hampshire	55,531	5,228	60,759	140	60,899
New Jersey	290,376	15,922	306,298	10,123	316,421
New York	1,151,563	121,423	1,636,996	18,648	1,655,644
North Carolina	298,206	481	298,687	203,820	502,507
Ohio	1,017,911	38,081	1,055,992	26,984	1,082,976
Oregon	57,940	1,783	59,728	2,166	61,894
Pennsylvania	1,333,311	64,076	1,397,387	24,990	1,422,377
Rhode Island	49,891	7,190	57,081	1,251	58,332
South Carolina	94,212	238	94,450	167,829	262,279
Tennessee	414,551	1,343	415,894	155,359	571,263
Texas	175,001	7,526	182,527	69,009	251,586
Vermont	93,006	6,080	99,086	377	99,463
Virginia	325,601	1,453	326,054	258,988	585,042
West Virginia	216,268	1,436	217,704	9,457	227,161
Wisconsin	448,708	51,281	499,989	2,224	502,218
Total	13,135,149	697,138	13,932,287	2,219,996	16,052,283
Arizona	5,296	2,622	7,918	1,653	9,571
Dakota	27,697	11,395	39,092	650	39,742
District of Columbia	29,011	561	29,592	13,945	43,537
Idaho	8,214	634	8,848	267	9,115
Montana	7,752	502	8,254	1,067	9,321
New Mexico	26,026	726	26,752	2,503	29,255
Utah	38,596	4,636	43,232	282	48,514
Washington	20,874	1,162	22,036	2,603	24,639
Wyoming	3,392	583	3,925	187	4,112
Total	166,858	22,791	189,619	23,157	212,806
Grand total	13,302,007	719,929	14,021,936	2,243,153	16,265,089

a Including Oriental and Indian.

TABLE III—*The illiteracy of white adults in 1880.*

States and Territories.	White persons 21 years of age and upward.			White males 21 years of age and upward.			White females 21 years of age and upward.		
	Enumerated.	Returned as unable to write.		Enumerated.	Returned as unable to write.		Enumerated.	Returned as unable to write.	
	No.	No.	Per cent.	No.	No.	Per cent.	No.	No.	Per cent.
Maine	376,382	16,?31	4.3	186,659	8,420	4.5	189,723	7,814	4.1
New Hampshire	215,706	10,694	5.0	104,901	5,264	5.0	110,805	5,430	4.9
Vermont	191,593	12,872	6.7	95,307	6,731	7.1	96,286	6,141	6.4
Massachusetts	1,051,684	81,671	7.8	496,692	30,951	6.2	554,992	50,720	9.1
Rhode Island	158,522	18,611	11.7	75,012	7,157	9.5	83,510	11,454	13.7
Connecticut	858,679	23,339	6.5	173,759	9,501	5.5	184,920	13,838	7.5
New York	2,826,859	182,050	6.4	1,388,692	76,745	5.5	1,488,167	105,305	7.8
New Jersey	587,736	87,848	6.4	289,965	15,902	6.5	297,771	21,446	7.2
Pennsylvania	2,151,246	174,286	8.1	1,070,392	65,985	6.2	1,080,854	108,301	10.0
Ohio	1,588,507	92,616	5.6	804,971	40,373	5.0	783,636	52,243	6.7
Michigan	848,590	48,291	5.7	461,557	26,330	5.7	387,033	21,961	5.7
Indiana	941,763	77,076	8.2	487,698	33,757	6.9	454,065	43,319	9.5
Wisconsin	637,221	45,798	7.2	338,932	21,221	6.3	298,289	24,577	8.2
Illinois	1,481,945	99,356	6.7	783,161	44,536	5.7	698,784	54,820	7.8
Minnesota	372,591	27,645	7.4	212,399	12,372	5.8	160,192	15,273	9.5
Iowa	768,677	35,815	4.7	413,633	16,202	3.9	355,044	19,613	5.5
Nebraska	216,924	7,821	3.6	128,198	3,836	3.0	88,726	3,985	4.5
Kansas	447,526	17,095	3.8	254,949	7,998	3.1	192,577	9,097	4.7
Northern Division	15,222,151	1,008,618	6.6	7,716,777	433,281	5.6	7,455,374	575,337	7.7
Delaware	63,032	6,462	10.3	31,902	2,955	9.3	31,130	3,507	11.3
Maryland	371,698	34,155	9.2	183,522	15,152	8.3	188,176	19,003	10.1
District of Columbia	65,681	3,569	5.4	31,955	1,350	4.2	33,726	2,219	6.6
Virginia	425,224	71,004	16.7	206,248	31,474	15.3	218,976	39,530	18.1
West Virginia	251,681	45,340	17.8	152,777	19,055	14.4	128,904	26,285	20.4
Kentucky	623,438	124,723	20.0	317,579	54,956	17.3	305,859	69,767	22.8
North Carolina	405,082	116,43	28.7	189,73.	44,420	23.4	215,350	72,017	33.4
Tennessee	507,413	118,734	23.4	250,05	46,948	18.8	257,358	71,786	27.9
South Carolina	182,518	34,335	18.8	86,90	13,924	16.0	95,618	20,411	21.3
Georgia	370,984	71,693	19.3	177,967	28,571	16.1	193,017	43,122	22.3
Alabama	294,941	60,174	20.4	141,461	24,150	17.3	153,480	35,724	23.3
Florida	65,713	10,885	16.6	34,210	4,706	13.8	31,503	6,179	19.6
Mississippi	214,122	27,789	13.0	108,254	12,473	11.5	105,868	15,316	14.5
Missouri	940,668	80,994	9.6	508,165	40,655	8.0	482,503	49,269	11.4
Arkansas	254,461	50,235	19.7	136,150	21,349	15.7	118,311	28,886	24.4
Louisiana	213,172	31,813	16.3	108,810	16,377	15.1	104,362	18,436	17.7
Texas	534,783	65,117	12.2	301,737	33,085	11.0	233,046	32,032	17.7
Southern Division	5,791,617	965,389	16.6	2,867,421	411,90	14.3	2,847,187	553,489	19.4
California	424,636	22,626	5.3	262,583	12,616	4.8	162,053	10,010	6.2
Oregon	81,826	2,904	3.5	51,636	1,669	3.2	30,190	1,235	4.1
Nevada	34,952	1,807	5.2	25,633	1,173	4.6	9,319	634	6.8
Colorado	125,131	7,025	5.6	92,088	3,627	3.9	33,043	3,398	10.3
Arizona	23,125	3,55-	15.4	18,046	2,150	11.9	5,079	1,400	27.6
Washington	35,614	1,011	2.8	24,251	642	2.6	11,363	369	3.2
Idaho	16,023	510	3.2	11,609	319	2.7	4,351	191	4.4
Utah	60,681	5,385	8.9	32,078	2,137	6.7	28,603	3,248	11.4
Montana	24,311	525	2.2	19,636	410	2.1	4,675	115	2.5
Dakota	74,629	3,206	4.3	50,962	1,678	3.3	23,667	1,528	6.5
Wyoming	12,327	285	2.3	9,211	160	1.7	3,086	125	4.1
New Mexico	54,185	33,623	62.1	36,951	14,898	48.3	28,201	18,725	8.7
Pacific Division	967,440	82,456	8.5	628,854	41,475	6.6	338,636	40,978	12.1
Grand total	21,984,202	2,056,463	9.4	11,343,400	886,659	7.8	10,611,197	1,169,804	11.0

54 Appendix.

TABLE IV.—The illiteracy of colored adults in 1880.

States and Territories.	Colored persons of 21 years of age and upward. Enumerated. No.	Returned as unable to write. No.	Per cent.	Colored males of 21 years of age and upward. Enumerated. No.	Returned as unable to write. No.	Per cent.	Colored females of 21 years of age and upward. Enumerated. No.	Returned as unable to write. No.	Per cent.
Maine	1,238	335	27.1	664	144	21.7	574	191	33.3
New Hampshire	448	81	18.1	237	42	17.7	211	39	18.5
Vermont	541	129	23.8	314	82	26.1	227	47	20.7
Massachusetts	12,026	2,221	18.5	5,956	941	15.8	6,070	1,280	21.1
Rhode Island	4,221	1,139	27.0	1,886	467	21.8	2,345	672	28.8
Connecticut	7,239	1,497	20.7	3,522	696	19.7	3,707	801	21.6
New York	44,318	10,31	24.5	20,059	4,521	22.5	21,289	5,613	26.4
New Jersey	21,924	7,814	35.8	10,670	3,560	33.4	11,251	4,284	38.1
Pennsylvania	43,869	15,551	31.8	23,892	6,845	28.6	24,977	8,706	31.9
Ohio	40,940	14,152	34.6	21,706	7,011	32.4	19,234	7,111	37.0
Michigan	11,417	3,758	32.9	6,130	1,852	30.2	5,287	1,906	36.1
Indiana	19,834	8,806	41.4	10,739	4,345	40.5	9,095	4,461	49.0
Wisconsin	2,857	981	34.3	1,550	471	30.6	1,307	507	38.8
Illinois	24,327	10,397	42.7	13,686	5,271	38.8	10,641	5,126	48.2
Minnesota	1,945	769	39.5	1,086	364	33.5	859	405	47.1
Iowa	5,228	1,958	37.5	3,125	1,009	33.4	2,203	949	43.1
Nebraska	1,424	496	34.8	844	256	30.3	580	240	41.4
Kansas	20,315	11,498	56.6	10,765	5,623	52.2	9,550	5,875	61.5
Northern Division	266,188	91,746	31.9	136,741	43,533	31.8	129,397	4,213	38.0
Delaware	12,658	7,935	62.7	6,396	3,787	59.2	6,262	4,148	66.2
Maryland	100,107	66,357	66.3	48,584	30,873	63.5	51,523	35,484	68.9
District of Columbia	32,777	19,447	59.3	13,918	7,520	54.0	18,859	11,927	63.2
Virginia	267,612	214,310	80.1	128,257	100,210	78.1	139,355	114,130	81.9
West Virginia	11,899	7,539	64.4	6,384	3,830	60.0	5,515	3,709	67.3
Kentucky	120,349	90,738	75.4	58,642	43,177	74.6	61,707	47,561	77.1
North Carolina	215,619	174,152	80.8	105,015	80,282	76.4	110,631	93,870	81.8
Tennessee	166,839	126,939	76.1	80,250	58,601	73.0	86,589	68,338	78.9
South Carolina	241,129	200,063	81.9	118,889	93,010	78.2	125,240	107,053	85.5
Georgia	293,421	247,318	84.3	143,471	116,516	81.2	149,950	130,802	87.2
Alabama	246,075	206,878	84.1	118,423	96,408	81.4	127,652	110,470	86.5
Florida	53,897	39,755	73.8	27,489	19,110	69.5	26,408	20,643	78.2
Mississippi	262,744	208,122	79.2	130,278	99,068	76.0	132,466	109,054	82.3
Missouri	66,321	40,35	60.9	33,042	19,025	57.6	33,279	21,329	64.1
Arkansas	88,690	68,444	77.2	46,827	34,300	73.2	41,86	34,144	81.6
Louisiana	218,167	178,789	82.0	107,977	86,555	80.2	110,190	92,234	83.7
Texas	155,069	121,827	78.6	88,639	59,669	75.9	76,430	62,158	81.3
Southern Division	2,556,103	2,018,998	78.9	1,252,481	951,944	76.0	1,303,919	1,067,054	81.9
California	75,189	22,100	29.4	66,889	16,857	25.2	8,330	5,243	62.6
Oregon	8,651	2,387	27.6	7,993	2,005	25.1	6,8	382	58.1
Nevada	6,653	1,638	24.6	5,622	1,194	21.2	1,031	444	43.1
Colorado	2,142	465	21.7	1,520	289	19.0	622	176	28.3
Arizona	3,075	633	20.6	2,352	422	17.9	723	211	29.2
Washington	4,553	1,844	41.4	3,419	1,126	32.9	1,134	758	66.8
Idaho	3,288	943	28.7	3,126	869	27.8	162	74	45.7
Utah	958	518	54.1	695	356	51.2	263	162	61.6
Montana	2,341	777	33.6	1,908	483	25.3	473	291	62.3
Dakota	1,085	458	42.2	641	2,0	32.8	444	248	55.9
Wyoming	1,078	144	13.4	939	84	8.9	139	6,4	43.2
New Mexico	5,641	5,209	92.3	3,095	2,779	89.8	2,546	2,430	95.4
Pacific Division	114,694	37,156	33.2	98,149	26,674	27.3	16,575	10,482	62.6
Grand total	2,937,235	2,147,900	73.1	1,487,344	1,022,151	68.7	1,449,891	1,125,749	77.6

TABLE V.—*The illiteracy of white adults in 1870.*

States and Territories.	White persons 21 years of age and upward.			White males 21 years of age and upward.			White females 21 years of age and upward.		
	Enumerated.	Returned as unable to write.		Enumerated.	Returned as unable to write.		Enumerated.	Returned as unable to write.	
	No.	No.	Per cent.	No.	No.	Per cent.	No.	No.	Per cent.
Maine	342,740	13,291	3.3	169,194	6,516	3.9	173,546	6,775	3.9
New Hampshire	189,830	7,586	4.0	90,840	3,361	8.7	98,990	4,225	4.3
Vermont	182,586	13,312	7.3	90,324	6,867	7.6	92,062	6,445	7.0
Massachusetts	829,495	83,812	10.1	394,047	30,920	7.8	435,448	52,890	12.1
Rhode Island	121,217	16,072	13.3	57,312	5,922	10.3	63,905	10,152	15.9
Connecticut	302,566	22,673	7.5	147,659	8,990	6.1	154,907	13,683	8.2
New York	2,325,130	189,952	8.2	1,146,004	71,208	6.4	1,179,126	116,744	9.9
New Jersey	458,380	36,431	8.0	228,984	14,515	6.5	229,896	21,916	9.6
Pennsylvania	1,698,109	177,611	10.5	848,790	61,30	7.2	849,319	116,261	13.6
Ohio	1,243,143	109,888	8.8	625,253	41,189	6.6	617,890	68,449	11.1
Michigan	580,896	35,529	6.1	311,718	17,543	5.6	269,178	17,986	6.7
Indiana	739,670	93,982	12.7	382,081	36,331	9.5	357,589	57,651	16.1
Wisconsin	478,521	40,307	8.4	254,262	17,647	6.9	224,259	22,660	10.1
Illinois	1,157,220	97,858	8.4	617,567	40,801	6.6	539,653	56,857	10.5
Minnesota	201,475	18,150	9.0	111,344	8,041	7.0	87,131	10,109	11.6
Iowa	532,957	34,607	6.5	289,179	11,782	5.1	243,778	19,825	8.1
Nebraska	61,681	2,125	3.4	38,784	956	2.5	22,897	1,169	5.1
Kansas	167,231	12,169	7.3	101,489	5,994	5.9	65,748	6,175	9.4
Northern Division	11,607,850	1,005,155	8.7	5,903,031	395,173	6.7	5,701,819	609,982	10.7
Delaware	49,996	8,032	16.1	24,811	3,466	14.0	25,185	4,566	18.1
Maryland	296,173	32,766	11.1	145,622	13,344	9.2	150,551	19,422	12.9
District of Columbia	47,089	8,756	8.4	23,178	1,214	5.2	23,911	2,342	10.6
Virginia	340,316	67,997	20.4	161,500	27,646	17.1	178,816	40,351	22.5
West Virginia	182,831	39,76	21.7	91,345	15,181	16.6	91,486	24,515	25.7
Kentucky	481,647	106,551	22.1	245,138	43,826	17.9	236,509	62,725	26.5
North Carolina	310,001	95,839	30.9	139,535	33,111	23.7	170,466	62,728	36.8
Tennessee	408,550	106,538	26.1	199,056	37,713	18.9	209,494	68,825	32.9
South Carolina	133,806	30,391	22.7	62,517	12,490	20.0	71,259	17,901	25.1
Georgia	278,534	62,430	22.4	129,665	21,899	16.9	148,869	40,531	27.2
Alabama	223,897	43,430	21.6	105,474	17,429	16.5	118,423	31,001	26.2
Florida	41,225	9,476	23.0	21,065	3,876	18.8	20,160	5,600	27.8
Mississippi	166,044	23,031	13.9	84,784	9,357	11.0	81,260	13,746	16.9
Missouri	710,467	84,904	11.9	384,324	31,780	9.0	326,143	50,124	15.4
Arkansas	148,661	35,380	23.8	77,195	13,610	17.6	71,366	21,770	30.5
Louisiana	167,993	27,588	16.4	87,066	12,048	14.0	80,927	15,540	19.2
Texas	241,350	37,350	15.5	132,390	17,505	13.2	108,960	19,845	18.2
Southern Division	4,228,480	820,257	19.4	2,114,615	318,495	15.1	2,113,755	501,762	23.7
California	281,230	22,199	7.9	186,823	12,362	6.6	94,407	9,837	10.4
Oregon	39,711	2,181	5.5	25,611	1,085	4.2	14,070	1,096	7.8
Nevada	29,285	600	2.0	24,266	474	1.1	5,019	126	2.5
Colorado	22,937	4,379	19.1	16,087	2,305	14.3	6,850	2,074	30.3
Arizona	6,673	1,934	29.0	5,311	1,167	22.0	1,362	767	56.3
Washington	11,824	616	5.2	8,773	437	5.0	3,051	179	5.9
Idaho	7,681	422	5.5	6,504	315	4.8	1,177	107	9.1
Utah	34,760	3,317	9.5	17,655	1,137	6.4	17,105	2,180	12.8
Montana	14,259	480	3.4	12,551	399	3.2	1,708	81	4.7
Dakota	7,551	709	9.3	5,496	403	7.3	2,055	306	14.9
Wyoming	6,904	412	6.4	5,908	326	5.5	996	86	8.6
New Mexico	42,262	32,027	75.8	23,177	14,892	64.3	19,085	17,135	89.8
Pacific Division	505,077	69,276	13.7	338,192	35,302	10.4	166,885	33,974	20.4
Grand total	16,341,407	1,894,688	11.6	8,355,918	748,970	9.0	7,985,489	1,145,718	14.4

TABLE VI.—*The illiteracy of colored adults in 1870.*

States and Territories	Colored persons of 21 years of age and upward.			Colored males of 21 years of age and upward.			Colored females of 21 years of age and upward.		
	Enumerated.	Returned as unable to write.		Enumerated.	Returned as unable to write.		Enumerated.	Returned as unable to write.	
	No.	No.	Per cent.	No.	No.	Per cent.	No.	No.	Per cent.
Maine	1,151	128	11.1	629	69	11.0	522	59	11.3
New Hampshire	341	70	20.5	182	38	20.9	159	32	20.1
Vermont	491	87	17.7	281	47	16.5	207	40	19.3
Massachusetts	8.440	1,876	22.2	4,126	826	20.0	4.314	1,050	24.3
Rhode Island	3,149	728	23.1	1,440	296	20.6	1,709	432	25.3
Connecticut	5.747	1,353	23.5	2,756	634	23.0	2,991	719	24.0
New York	30 668	8,873	29.0	14,737	3,952	26.8	15,931	4,923	30.9
New Jersey	16,134	6,393	39.0	7,879	2,882	36.6	8.255	3,511	42.5
Pennsylvania	35,661	13,232	37.1	17,093	5,760	33.7	18,571	7,472	40.2
Ohio	30,391	15,621	51.4	15,649	7,565	48.1	14,742	8,086	54.9
Michigan	7,858	3.243	41.1	4,226	1,532	36.2	3,632	1,701	46.8
Indiana	11,661	6,410	55.2	6 161	3,212	52.1	5,500	3,228	58.7
Wisconsin	1,656	469	27.8	897	211	27.2	769	219	28.5
Illinois	14,349	8,061	56.2	7,706	3,974	51.6	6,643	4,087	61.5
Minnesota	756	334	44.2	395	151	39.0	361	180	49.9
Iowa	2,792	1,340	46.9	1,556	635	40.8	1,236	675	54.6
Nebraska	479	157	32.8	298	96	32.2	181	61	33.7
Kansas	8,691	5,900	73.2	4,191	2,900	69.2	3,900	3,030	77.4
Northern Division	179,888	74,231	41.3	90,205	34,786	38.6	89,623	39,495	44.1
Delaware	10,481	7,970	76.0	5,224	3,765	72.1	5,257	4,205	80.0
Maryland	81,904	59,769	72.9	39,124	27,125	69.3	42,791	32,584	76.2
District of Columbia	23,195	18,356	79.1	10,151	7,599	74.9	13 044	10,757	82.5
Virginia	226 438	207,679	91.3	107,742	97,916	90.9	118,696	109,763	92.4
West Virginia	8,067	6,628	82.2	3,972	3,186	80.2	4,095	3,442	84.1
Kentucky	93,736	81,190	86.6	44,338	37,890	85.5	49,398	43,205	87.6
North Carolina	162 447	145,211	89.6	78,278	68,805	87.9	84,169	76,406	90.8
Tennessee	134,445	119,200	88.3	64,144	55,904	87.2	70,301	63,256	89.8
South Carolina	178 253	148,786	83.5	85,505	70 841	82.9	92,748	77,944	84.0
Georgia	225,198	212,973	94.1	1 7 975	10 556	98.1	117,223	112,867	95.9
Alabama	202,477	189,898	93.5	97,841	91,634	93.0	104,636	98,360	94.0
Florida	38,347	34,863	90.8	18,844	16,811	89.2	19,553	18,052	92.3
Mississippi	186,856	168,378	90.1	90,191	80,927	89.7	96 665	87,451	90.5
Missouri	44,487	34,604	78.0	23,892	18 008	74.1	25,59	20,596	80.5
Arkansas	52,389	46 382	88.5	26,888	23,685	88.1	25,501	22,697	89.0
Louisiana	176,337	1 6 317	88.6	87,121	76,772	83.1	89,216	79.545	89.2
Texas	103,118	74 949	92.1	51,704	47,314	91.5	51,494	47,635	92.7
Southern Division	1,953 215	1,736,538	88.9	942,933	829 212	87.8	1,010.282	908,826	89.9
California	46 143	4,164	9.0	40,862	2,899	7.1	5,281	1,265	24.0
Oregon	3,27	912	28.3	2,976	800	26.8	251	112	44.6
Nevada	2,959	191	6.5	2,675	176	6.6	284	15	5 3
Colorado	351	163	46 4	211	70	33.2	140	9	66.4
Arizona	52	15	28.8	42	10	23.8	10	5	50.0
Washington	1,051	355	33.8	510	85	14.7	541	270	49.9
Idaho	3,945	2 559	64.9	3,819	2,481	65.0	126	78	61.9
Utah	452	176	38.9	388	159	41.0	64	17	26.6
Montana	2,07	222	10.8	1,879	150	8.0	196	72	36.7
Dakota	518	371	71.8	228	153	67.1	29	218	75.2
Wyoming	252	91	36.1	199	57	28.6	53	34	64.1
New Mexico	423	470	89.9	156	139	89.1	367	331	90.2
Pacific Division	61,548	9,689	15 7	53,915	7,179	13.3	7 603	2,510	33.1
Grand total	2,194,591	1,820,508	83.0	1,087,683	870,177	80.0	1,107,508	930,311	85.8

TABLE VII—*The illiteracy of white and colored persons 10 or more years old in 1870.*

States and Territories.	White persons 10 years of age and upward.			Colored persons 10 years of age and upwards.		
	Enumerated.	Returned as unable to write.		Enumerated.	Returned as unable to write	
	Number	Number.	Per cent.	Number.	Number.	Per cent.
Maine	492,128	18,874	3.8	1,719	178	10.3
New Hampshire	259,9?3	9,831	3.8	522	95	18.2
Vermont	257,99?	17,584	6.8	758	122	16.1
Massachusetts	1,148,99?	95,578	8.3	11,676	2,164	18.5
Rhode Island	169,479	21,029	12.4	4,272	892	20.9
Connecticut	4?7,804	27,913	6.7	8,?92	1,703	21.0
New York	3,336,198	228,424	6.8	42,761	10,847	25.4
New Jersey	656,972	46,386	7.1	23,715	8,301	35.4
Pennsylvania	2,516,344	206,458	8.1	51,465	15,898	30.9
Ohio	1,906,494	152,383	8.0	46,880	20,789	44.3
Michigan	861,523	48,649	5.6	12,240	4,478	36.6
Indiana	1,179,792	118,761	10.1	18,114	8,363	46.1
Wisconsin	749,181	54,845	7.3	2,524	596	23.6
Illinois	1,788,175	123,624	6.9	21,431	9,960	46.5
Minnesota	304,418	28,941	7.9	1,150	472	41.0
Iowa	833,698	44,145	5.3	4,261	1,526	35.8
Nebraska	87,562	4,630	5.3	703	231	32.9
Kansas	245,267	16,978	6.9	12,784	7,572	59.1
Northern Division	17,241,929	1,260,033	7.3	265,096	94,187	35.5
Delaware	76,016	11,280	14.8	16,570	11,820	71.3
Maryland	447,731	46,792	10.4	127,708	88,707	69.5
District of Columbia	66,620	4,876	7.3	33,833	23,843	70.5
Virginia	527,432	123,588	23.4	362,624	322,355	88.9
Kentucky	295,519	71,493	24.2	12,905	9,997	77.4
West Virginia	773,653	201,077	26.0	156,183	131,099	83.8
North Carolina	497,132	166,397	34.5	272,497	231,293	84.8
Tennessee	665,390	178,727	26.9	225,482	185,970	82.4
South Carolina	213,794	55,167	25.8	289,969	235,212	81.1
Georgia	462,718	124,939	27.0	373,211	343,654	92.1
Alabama	377,967	92,059	24.4	328,835	290,953	88.1
Florida	68,371	18,904	27.6	62,748	52,899	84.1
Mississippi	276,132	48,028	17.4	305,074	265,282	87.0
Missouri	1,122,17?	161,763	14.4	83,393	60,648	72.7
Arkansas	?56,48?	64,095	25.0	85,249	69,244	81.2
Louisiana	264,0?.	50,749	19.2	262,359	225,409	85.9
Texas	401,11?	70,895	17.7	169,965	150,808	88.7
Southern Division	6,792,28?	1,490,779	21.9	3,168,905	2,699,193	85.2
California	372,493	26,158	7.0	57,951	5,558	9.6
Oregon	60,846	3,411	5.6	3,839	1,016	26.5
Nevada	33,175	653	2.0	3,480	219	6.3
Colorado	29,819	6,564	22.0	530	259	48.9
Arizona	8,170	2,729	33.3	67	24	35.8
Washington	15,873	823	5.2	1,461	484	33.1
Idaho	8,839	486	5.5	4,350	2,902	66.7
Utah	55,828	7,097	12.7	687	266	38.7
Montana	15,925	643	4.0	2,245	275	12.2
Dakota	9,766	914	9.4	874	649	74.3
Wyoming	7,709	481	6.2	350	121	34.6
New Mexico	65,224	51,140	78.4	1,240	1,080	87.1
Pacific Division	688,667	101,099	14.8	77,074	12,853	16.7
Grand total	24,717,5?0	2,851,911	11.5	3,511,075	2,806,233	79.9

TABLE VIII.—*The illiteracy of white and colored persons* 10 *or more years old in* 1880.

States and Territories.	White persons 10 years of age and upward.			Colored persons 10 years of age and upward.		
	Enumerated.	Returned as unable to write.		Enumerated.	Returned as unable to write.	
	Number.	Number.	Per cent.	Number.	Number.	Per cent.
Maine	518,011	21,758	4.2	1,658	412	24.8
New Hampshire	285,594	14,208	5.0	594	94	15.8
Vermont	263,245	15,681	6.0	807	156	19.3
Massachusetts	1,416,767	90,658	6.4	15,416	2,322	15.1
Rhode Island	215,158	23,544	10.9	5,303	1,249	23.6
Connecticut	487,780	26,763	5.5	9,528	1,661	17.4
New York	3,927,608	208,175	5.3	53,825	11,425	21.2
New Jersey	835,385	44,049	5.3	30,206	9,200	30.5
Pennsylvania	3,136,561	209,981	6.7	66,654	18,033	27.1
Ohio	2,339,528	115,491	4.9	59,839	16,356	27.3
Michigan	1,219,906	58,932	4.8	16,780	4,791	28.5
Indiana	1,438,955	100,398	7.0	29,140	10,363	35.6
Wisconsin	961,438	54,233	5.6	4,279	1,325	31.0
Illinois	2,234,478	132,426	5.9	34,837	12,971	37.2
Minnesota	557,183	33,506	6.0	2,794	1,040	37.2
Iowa	1,174,068	44,337	3.8	7,578	2,272	30.0
Nebraska	316,312	10,926	3.5	1,959	602	30.7
Kansas	673,121	24,888	3.7	31,176	14,588	46.8
Northern Division	22,091,083	1,239,954	5.5	372,368	108,870	29.2
Delaware	91,611	8,346	9.1	19,245	11,068	57.5
Maryland	544,086	44,816	8.1	151,278	90,172	59.6
District of Columbia	91,872	3,988	4.3	45,045	21,790	48.4
Virginia	630,684	114,692	18.2	428,450	315,660	73.7
West Virginia	410,141	75,237	18.3	18,446	10,189	55.0
Kentucky	973,275	214,497	22.0	190,223	133,895	70.4
North Carolina	608,806	192,032	31.5	351,145	271,943	77.4
Tennessee	791,744	216,227	27.3	271,386	194,495	71.7
South Carolina	272,706	59,777	21.9	394,750	310,071	78.5
Georgia	563,977	1/8,934	22.9	479,863	391,432	81.6
Alabama	452,722	111,767	24.7	399,058	321,680	80.6
Florida	99,137	19,763	19.9	85,518	60,420	70.7
Mississippi	328,296	53,448	16.3	425,397	519,753	75.2
Missouri	1,453,238	152,510	10.5	104,393	56,244	53.9
Arkansas	398,905	98,542	25.0	137,971	103,473	75.0
Louisiana	320,917	58,951	18.4	328,153	259,429	79.1
Texas	808,931	123,912	15.3	255,265	192,520	75.4
Southern Division	8,834,948	1,676,939	18.9	4,085,571	3,064,234	75.0
California	589,235	26,090	4.4	91,857	27,340	29.8
Oregon	119,482	4,343	3.6	11,083	3,080	27.8
Nevada	42,595	1,915	4.5	8,071	2,154	26.7
Colorado	155,456	9,966	6.4	2,764	568	20.5
Arizona	28,634	4,824	16.8	4,288	1,018	23.7
Washington	49,269	1,429	2.9	6,451	2,460	38.1
Idaho	21,481	784	3.6	3,524	994	28.2
Utah	95,876	8,137	8.5	1,318	689	52.3
Montana	28,986	631	2.2	3,003	1,076	35.8
Dakota	98,348	4,157	4.2	1,501	664	44.2
Wyoming	15,240	374	2.5	1,239	182	14.7
New Mexico	79,767	49,597	62.2	8,199	7,559	92.2
Pacific Division	1,324,369	112,187	8.4	143,268	47,781	33.4
Grand total	32,130,400	3,019,080	9.4	4,601,207	3,220,878	70.0

TABLE IX—*Showing total valuation of real estate and personal property, valuation per capita, public indebtedness (not national) taxation and total expenditures on public schools as shown for 1880 in the Tenth Census.*

NEW ENGLAND STATES.	Assessed valuation.	Valuation per capita.	Debts.	Taxation.	Expenditures.
1. Maine	$235,978,716	$363 63	$ 22,466,850	$ 5,182,135	$ 991,297
5. New Hampshire..............	164,755,181	474 81	10,724,176	2,697,640	568,108
3. Vermont....................	86,806,775	261 24	4,352,168	1,745,111	452,693
4. Massachusetts..............	1,584,756 802	888 77	91,283,918	24,326,877	4,720,951
5. Rhode Island..............	252,536,673	913 22	13,104,790	2,602,715	530,167
6. Connecticut...............	327,177.532	525 4'	22,001,661	5,865,739	1,335,234
Total...................	2,652,011,532	661 26	163,871,552	42,010,217	8,598,446
MIDDLE STATES.					
1. New York..................	2,651,910,006	521 74	218,723,314	56,392,975	9,936,662
2. New Jersey................	572,518,361	506 15	49,517,102	8,958,065	2,039,938
3. Pennsylvania..............	1,683,459,016	393 06	111,034,759	28,601,334	7,306,692
4. Delaware..................	59,951,643	403 92	2,316,585	601,257	172,455
5. Maryland..................	497,307,675	531 91	10,896,006	5,437,462	1,395,284
6. District of Columbia......	99,401,787	559 51	· 22,675,459	1,469,254	438,567
Total..................	5,564,578,483	477 39	118,223,225	101,466,347	21,289,578
SOUTHERN STATES.					
1. Virginia.................	308,455,135	203 92	42,099,802	4,642.202	889,862
2. West Virginia............	139,622,705	225 75	1,513,424	2,056,979	720,967
3. North Carolina...........	156,100,202	111 52	8,144,606	1,916,132	383,709
4. South Carolina...........	133,560,135	134 15	13,345,938	1,839,983	367,259
5. Georgia.................	239,472,599	155 28	19,681,903	3,207,008	653,464
6. Florida.................	30,938,309	114 80	2,626,509	605,180	117,724
7. Alabama.................	122,867,228	97 32	14,728,545	2,061,978	430,131
8. Mississippi	110,628,129	97 76	2,013,190	2,884,475	679,475
9. Louisiana...............	160,162,439	170 39	42,865,952	4,395,876	455,758
10. Texas..................	320,364,515	201 26	11,604,913	4,568,716	782,735
11. Arkansas..............	86,409,364	107 67	7,938,784	1,839,099	382,637
12. Kentucky..............	350,563,971	212 63	14,977,881	5,201,017	1,162,944
13. Tennessee.............	211,778,538	137 30	37,387,900	2,788,781	786,088
Total.................	2,370,923,269	155 39	218,979,347	37,507,417	7,812,693
WESTERN STATES.					
1. Ohio...................	1,584,360,505	479 77	48,756,454	25,756,658	7,707,670
2. Indiana...............	727,815,131	367 89	18,354 737	10,843,680	4,504,407
3. Illinois.............	786,616,394	255 57	41 912,422	19,283,413	7,536,682
4. Michigan.............	517,666,359	316 24	8,803,144	8,627,949	3,112,463
5 Wisconsin............	438,971,751	333 69	11,876,992	5,838,325	2,163,845
6. Iowa................	398,671,251	245 89	7,962,767	10,261,605	4,347,119
7. Minnesota...........	258,028,687	330 47	8,476,064	3,713,707	1,622,919
8. Missouri............	532,795,801	245 71	57,487,664	10,269,736	3,092,332
9. Kansas.............	160,891,689	161 52	16,006,858	4,414,821	1,810,561
10. Nebraska...........	90,585,782	260 23	7,425,757	2,792,480	1,079,966
11. Colorado...........	74,471,693	383 22	3,594,296	2,152,008	400,205
12. Nevada.............	29,291,459	470 42	1,024,523	871,673	2 2,164
13. Oregon	52,522,084	300 52	848,502	1,113,942	316,835
14. California	584,578,036	676 05	16,755,688	12,628,005	3,031,014
Total................	6,187,266,625	333 26	252,314,583	118,567,952	40,917,497
TERRITORIES.					
1. Arizona.............	9,270,214	229 23	377,501	293,036	61,172
2. Dakota.............	20,321,530	150 33	993,860	478,066	183,257
3. Idaho.............	6,440,876	197 51	235,319	195,887	38,411
4. Montana..........	18,609,802	475 28	759,925	388,917	68,002
5. New Mexico.......	11,363,406	95 03	84,872	126,942	28,973
6. Utah..	24,775,279	172 09	116,251	435,238	179,887
7. Washington	23,810,693	316 9*	239,811	505,417	112,615
8. Wyoming..........	13,621,829	655 24	205,462	230,228	28,504
Total........	123,213,629	211 2	3,017,501	2,648,761	700,291
Grand Total........	$16,902,993,543	....	31,056,406,208	$302,20069 4	$79,339,814

www.ingramcontent.com/pod-product-compliance
Lightning Source LLC
Chambersburg PA
CBHW030720110426
42739CB00030B/1005